openhearted

openhearted

*eighty years of love, loss,
laughter and letting go*

ANN INGLE

SANDYCOVE

an imprint of

PENGUIN BOOKS

SANDYCOVE

UK | USA | Canada | Ireland | Australia
India | New Zealand | South Africa

Sandycove is part of the Penguin Random House group of companies
whose addresses can be found at global.penguinrandomhouse.com.

First published 2021
001

Copyright © Ann Ingle, 2021

The moral right of the author has been asserted

Set in 13.5/16pt Garamond MT Std
Typeset by Jouve (UK), Milton Keynes
Printed and bound in Great Britain by Clays Ltd, Elcograf S.p.A.

The authorized representative in the EEA is Penguin Random House Ireland,
Morrison Chambers, 32 Nassau Street, Dublin D02 YH68

A CIP catalogue record for this book is available from the British Library

ISBN: 978–1–844–88571–8

www.greenpenguin.co.uk

to
the man who loved me the best,
Peter Ingle

beginning

How do you start a book about your life? I went to a memoir-writing course and I still don't know the answer to that question. I sat, Wednesday afternoon after Wednesday afternoon, in a room in the Irish Writers Centre, with a group of people like me, in the third acts of our lives, discussing how to put those lives on the page.

When she read my pieces the tutor said that I should keep going. She said I had a voice. I liked that. I liked the idea of her reading my words and hearing my voice.

I still don't know the right way to begin. I mean, how does anything begin? It just does. So here I am. Beginning.

Ann Ingle. Born in London. Lately of Dublin. Beginning.

At eighty-one the idea of just beginning seems a little far-fetched. If life is a marathon, I am about to cross the finishing line. If life is a movie, the credits are soon to roll. If life . . . sorry, maybe I focused too much on metaphor while on that memoir-writing course. But you get my point. I am very far along in years; I've had more than my biblical three score and ten. And yet, somehow, it appears I am not finished.

To quote the brilliant American singer Amanda Palmer, 'I haven't finished yet. I still have a tattoo to get' – a tattoo that says *I wrote a memoir*.

I am eighty-one and the voice in my head says, 'Stupid old woman. Why do you think anyone will be interested in your life and what you have to say about anything?'

As we notch up those birthday milestones, as the

3

decades pass, we come to expect that a cloak of invisibility wraps around us. A cloak of irrelevance.

I am eighty-one and earlier this year, during lockdown, I learned how to do the cryptic crossword. I knitted a hat for the first time.

I am still maturing. I haven't finished yet.

And I refuse to wear that cloak. You can give it to someone else.

One Sunday, I was in a taxi on my way to my daughter's house. I often walk there along the Royal Canal but it was cold and rainy, so I called a taxi. This was in the olden days, the time before face masks and social distancing. The days when you could sit in the passenger seat.

Some of my children don't like me to sit in the passenger seat. They feel I am safer in the back. But I always enjoy talking to people, even taxi drivers, and I prefer not to sit in the back seat. It reminds me of that film, *Driving Miss Daisy*.

So this day, aged seventy-nine, I was sitting beside the taxi man going to visit one of my children for Sunday dinner.

The taxi driver heard my accent. Sixty years away from London and I still can't shake it. The taxi driver asked me where I came from. I told him.

He was one of the chatty ones and asked if I was married and where was my husband. I told the driver that he had been dead for thirty-nine years. He asked did we have children and I told him, 'Yes, we had eight children.'

'You dirty bitch,' he said. And he laughed.

I am not a bitch, dirty or otherwise. I am a woman who enjoyed sex and wanted a large family. Sex for me was never dirty. Having eight beautiful children was not dirty. The fact that anyone would suggest such a thing was disgusting. But I couldn't tell the taxi driver any of that. I just sat, silently seething, embarrassed and angry, until I arrived at my destination.

I didn't use my voice then. I'll use it now.

Something no one bothers to tell you is that when you get old, you fall.

Oh, you hear about it in passing, of course.

She had a fall, poor thing.

He tripped, yes, in front of Tesco. Went down head first.

I am not saying only older people fall, just that it's harder for us to get up when we do. And falling is not something you ever think about as a young woman. You think about falling in love. Falling for a film star. Falling pregnant. (What a strange phrase. But in my day you *fell* pregnant.)

You know things are changing, the first time you fall. And you always remember your first time.

My first fall was in the cinema in Belfast nearly twenty years ago, going to watch *A Beautiful Mind* with my daughter. I fell before the film even started, on the way up to my seat. I fell up the stairs, stairs that were lit like an airport runway at night. *Silly old woman*, I thought to myself. *Silly old woman falling upstairs*. I broke my left shoulder that time.

I grew more worried about falling as my eyes deteriorated. I was diagnosed with macular degeneration. Judi Dench has it. I felt better when I heard that. I don't know why.

In the last few years, I've had to stop reading books and start listening to them instead. It's not as terrible as it sounds. My reading life, in a way, became richer. Listening to books is still reading books, although some people are snooty about it. For me, it adds another dimension. How I have loved listening to Timothy West reading *The Way We Live Now* by Anthony Trollope or Gemma Whelan reading *Reasons to be Cheerful* by Nina Stibbe or Bríd Brennan reading *Milkman* by Anna Burns. I could go on.

The next time I fell it was in the opposite direction, downwards, which made more sense. ('Fall, fall again, fall better,' as Beckett might have put it.) I fell down a steep set of stairs, taking out the bins in the office of the local community newspaper I used to run.

I lay at the bottom of the stairs willing my arm to move, willing it to reach for my mobile phone, which was in my pocket. My arm wouldn't move. And yet as I lay there something surreal happened. I watched as my arm moved, exactly as I had willed it to. At the same time, I saw my unmoving arm, still inert on the floor. It was weird.

I was in hospital for a week that time. They put a metal plate in my shoulder and I vowed I would never fall again.

I fell again. A few years later. It was the morning I was rushing to see my daughter Róisín's newborn twins in Holles Street hospital. I damaged my ankle that time and arrived at Róisín's side in a wheelchair. She thought I was joking. Some joke.

Stupid old woman. More broken bones.

My sister, Joyce, emailed to remind me that she has broken her shoulder five times, once in a shop in Paris. 'It's not a competition,' I told her.

In 2020 I fell again, during the second lockdown. It was seven in the morning. I walked across the kitchen to find out which episode of *Horrible Histories* my little granddaughter Síofra was looking at. She had head-phones on, the wire curling from her ears down to the socket close to the ground. As I turned away to go back to my cup of tea, I tripped over the headphone wire. I fell heavily on the floor while Síofra cried. I tried and failed to get up and, despite everyone's best efforts to help, I had to wriggle over to the back door-step on my bottom before they managed to haul me to my feet.

The more you fall, the harder it is to get up.

*

In the Swiftcare clinic, which was not as swift as I hoped, the doctor spoke to my daughter and not to me about my smashed shoulder.

I had to visit the dentist a few days later and my son-in-law escorted me. There were stairs to climb and I took his arm gratefully. When we entered the surgery, the receptionist looked at us and said to him, 'Is she behaving herself for you?'

I thought about my friend, same age as me, in the supermarket the other day. At the till, her credit card would not work. The young member of staff who came up to her asked, too loudly, assuming my friend was hard of hearing, 'Is there someone with you, dear?' She assumed that my friend, an independent woman, had a carer. The young woman in the supermarket didn't mean anything bad by it, but it was another reminder.

'We are old now, everyone can see it,' I told my friend.

People make assumptions about us because of our grey hair and our slow-moving gait. Sometimes they don't see us at all. And, really, what else should we expect?

I met Peter in Newquay, Cornwall. I was a Londoner, he was a Dubliner. It shouldn't have worked but it did. Like magic. He put a spell on me, as the song goes. Peter could sing like a pop star, like an opera singer, like an angel.

We had eight children. We raised them – or, truthfully, I raised them – in a house in Sandymount village on the southside of Dublin. We lived facing a green full of trees. We lived so close to the sea that I could pack the children off to have their Sunday dinner, from tinfoil parcels, on the beach.

What am I doing here? Am I trying to write my dead husband back to life?

No, I am not trying to do that. Peter Ingle died forty-one years ago in 1980. He was forty-one when he died. I was forty-one when he died.

I coped after he went – I thought it was coping, anyway – by going on a bit of a rampage. I spent time with unsuitable men. I kept busy. I attacked the grief. Banished the pain. And within three or four years, the ghost of Peter Ingle no longer haunted me. It was sad. The saddest thing I've ever known. But my life did not end when Peter's did. There were more acts to follow.

And I wish I could tell you that I sometimes imagine our lives together now, if he had not died. Long drives in the countryside. A reassuring hand on my back after one of my falls. But I don't. Not because I didn't love him very much. I loved him like the greatest love story ever told. But when he died, I did not carry his shadow around. I was able to move on from the grief. I had to because there was a show to be kept on the road. And I was the one who had to do it.

I don't dream about him. Or rarely, anyway. I see him, though. In the way my son Peter walks, the curl in

Sarah's hair or when Róisín sings. He was the love of my life, but he is not a ghost in my life. In the last years, he suffered, and we endured that suffering together. I survived, moved through and past it, but Peter did not. And as I get close to the finishing line, I have come to believe that the illumination of his life and suffering might be meaningful.

I can't write him back to life. I wouldn't even if I could. But I can tell his story. Our story. My story. I can use my voice. I will use my voice.

nature boy

It began on a hot afternoon in July 1960. I was sunning myself on an embankment on the side of the road in Newquay, Cornwall, when a van stopped and out came a man and a dog.

Life is funny like that. There are no warnings or sign-posts in those seemingly ordinary moments, even as the entire course of your future and the future of your unborn children and their children is being decided. There are no thunderbolts, no voices bellowing from the clouds telling you to sit up and pay attention. Sometimes it's just a van stopping in front of you, transforming everything.

A man and a dog jumped out of the van. The dog ran over and began licking me, full of excitement. The owner of the dog apologized and introduced himself as Woody Zimmerman.

He was an American, he said. Of course he was. Woody Zimmerman was tall and very slender, and he had a ponytail of black greasy hair. As I sat petting the dog, he told me that he was looking for his friend. They had taken separate lifts from St Ives, some thirty miles away. Woody got a ride with the dog in a van, and his friend had hitched a lift in a car.

The American, the dog and I waited at the side of the road in the sunshine until his friend arrived. I had nothing else to do that sunny afternoon. Woody watched every car that passed and eventually stood up and lifted his arm to wave. A Ford Cortina stopped abruptly and out stepped his friend.

You might say it was a trick of the light or that my eyes were momentarily blinded by the sun, but there was an aura around the man who stepped out of that Ford Cortina. You can think what you like, but I saw it and I can still see it now: a dazzling light surrounding his mop of long, curly, blond hair. Michelangelo's David come to life.

I stood there at the side of the road beside Woody Zimmerman and his dog, and I fell in love.

Woody introduced us. 'This is Paddy,' he said.

Paddy was the first person from Ireland I had ever met and when he spoke his Irish accent was as beguiling and intriguing as he was. We sat talking for a while and Woody must have seen what was happening and said he would go and find somewhere to pitch the tent.

This Paddy person, the man who already had my heart, took my hand and said, 'Let's go for a walk.' So, we walked, hand in hand, rambling over the cliffs and gazing down at the roaring sea.

I was impressed by the way he talked from the very beginning, by his way of looking at things and really seeing them. As we walked over the rocks and sandy paths with seagulls and cormorants all around, he was saying 'look at that', 'see this', and he made me realize that I hadn't before, not really. I had never met anyone like him before or since. He was so natural, so real, somehow, and different. There was no pretence. He was just himself. Paddy.

And that was how it all started. A chance meeting on a sunny day in Cornwall.

The summer I met Paddy, I was enjoying my last months of freedom along with my beatnik friends – though I was only a part-time beatnik. When the sun shone and the holidays came, I donned my obligatory polo neck and headed for the hills – or, in this case, the seaside. But I didn't smoke dope or play the guitar. And I didn't come from a middle-class home as, I was later to find, most of them did.

I was a working-class girl and my parents were thrilled that I was the first of the family to go to college. I had left school at sixteen to work as a secretary. At nineteen I had returned to education so that I could become a teacher. My application to go to a teacher-training college in Leeds had been submitted. I was awaiting the results of my GCE[1] examination in the hope that I hadn't messed up too badly. My future seemed all set.

My friend Wendy and I were working part-time on the ice-cream counter at Woolworths in Newquay. You might not remember Woolworths, it's been gone a long time now. You could buy anything and everything all under one roof for half nothing.

In the morning I worked but the rest of the day was

---

1. General Certificate of Education, the entry-level qualification for tertiary education in England.

left for me and Paddy. I knew nothing about Ireland. He made it sound like a paradise of green fields, mountains and blue seas. He was telling the truth, it is a beautiful country.

We lay on the beach together and he sang to me, as only he could. His repertoire amazed me: songs from Frank Sinatra to Elvis, from Bill Haley to Mario Lanza. He sang folk songs too, about strange people and rebellion. Who was Biddy Mulligan and where was the Coombe? I longed to know. Those songs about Spanish ladies and black velvet bands were new to me. I was more used to hearing Woody Guthrie singing about peace and the common people of America or Pete Seeger singing 'We Shall Overcome'.

Paddy sang the rebel songs with passion. Kevin Barry and Willie McBride were names I was not familiar with. He told me that Britain had oppressed the Irish for eight hundred years, a proclamation I was to hear repeated many times over the coming years, and not just from him.

I apologized profusely on behalf of my fellow countrymen. Apparently, the British had subjugated the Irish for centuries, but it was news to me. I had studied history at school and, although the Empire and the valour of the British in the two world wars were covered extensively, Ireland was never mentioned. I don't feel so bad about it today. Those MPs in the Conservative Party discussing Brexit in 2016 were just as uninformed.

Apart from my ignorance of everything Irish, Paddy

and I had little to disagree about as we whiled away those sunny weeks. Day after day – foraging for food, cooking soup on the beach, telling stories, singing songs – life was idyllic. William Blake wrote:

> The tree which moves some to tears of joy is in the eyes of others only a green thing that stands in the way. Some see nature all ridicule and deformity . . . and some scarce see nature at all. But to the eyes of the man of imagination, nature is imagination itself.

> Paddy was a man of imagination.

I don't know if Paddy loved me from the beginning, but I believe during those few weeks together he saw me as a person who would be loving and forgiving. I saw in him someone who needed me, someone who might be misunderstood but who I would always understand. My love for him was and always would be unconditional as long as he wanted it.

As I write these words they sound so melodramatic, but there was something very special about those first days with him that I can't explain in any other way. He was different from the others around me and they didn't take to him. Paddy didn't buy into the pseudo-hippy scene because he was genuinely just himself, without any pretensions.

I had promised my parents that I would be home for my twenty-first birthday. I couldn't let them down and, besides, I had a job to go to. Before leaving London, I had been accepted as a teacher in a Pitman's College in Forest Gate. This was a great opportunity for me and good experience before I went to teacher-training college. Private colleges took on unqualified teachers in those days.

I had to say goodbye to this gorgeous boy and go home to blow up balloons, cut cake and cry into my fizzy wine. I had found the man of my dreams and now I had to leave him. Life can seem so unfair when you're twenty and in love for the very first time.

Paddy walked with me to the station and I gave him my telephone number. As I waved goodbye and he ran along the platform, I desperately hoped that this would not be my last sight of his beautiful face.

I picture myself like Celia Johnson in *Brief Encounter*, hanging out of that carriage window as she waved goodbye to Trevor Howard. I am such an old drama queen. My anguish was real, though. I couldn't bear the idea that this was all it was, a brief encounter. Just a summer love affair, a fling.

I arrived at Paddington Station with eyes red from crying.

I watched *The Great British Bake Off* last night on the television. The competitors had to bake a cake representing their twenty-first birthdays. If I had been a contestant, I would have made a heart-shaped cake, broken in two.

That's how I felt. Sad and broken. Paddy was far away and, as the weeks went by, I believed I would never see him again. You must remember that awful feeling of sadness when you think all is lost. Young love. You yearn for someone and they're not there. It's tragic.

But then, the telephone rang.

One Saturday in late October I picked up the receiver of the old black phone in the hall. It was Paddy.

After two months apart, we just picked up where we had left off. We met or talked on the phone every day after that. He and Woody had moved into a flat in Camden Town. The very place for an Irishman in search of digs.

Paddy was only the second man I had brought home to meet my parents. The first was a quiet boy who had just finished his National Service in the army and was picking me up to go to the cinema. When I introduced him, my father barely said hello, turned on his heels and went out into the back yard, whereupon he cried. Baby Ann all grown up and dating a boy was too much for him.

I was nervous when I brought Paddy home for Sunday lunch, but he wasn't, not one bit. Looking like a reincarnation of the Greek god Adonis, with his suntan and golden locks falling over his eyes, he sat at the table and ate all around him. He complimented my mother on her cooking and behaved as if he had been coming to dinner in our house for years.

I read somewhere that women are attracted to men who are like their fathers. If that's so, it's probably one of the few things my mother and I had in common. The man I was in love with and my father were both charismatic, blue-eyed charmers who loved a drink and a gamble.

After the meal, we played cards. Paddy dealt like Paul Newman in *Cool Hand Luke*, his big hands throwing the cards with ease and precision, and, of course, he won. 'The luck of the Irish,' my father muttered. My mother took to him because she loved the way he said her name: the 'th' in Ethel was transformed by his Irish accent.

My father was wary at first but a few pints together in the Hare and Hounds sorted that out – that and their mutual love of the noble art of boxing and Baby Ann.

Living at home was not working for either of us. Paddy came to the house in the evening, but we were never left on our own. My parents looked exhausted but that didn't stop them making excuses to stay up to watch something on the television. It was unbearable and so I left home.

I moved into a bedsit near Paddy, owned by a Catholic lady who, as I was paying the first week's rent, told me that the house was haunted by her dead husband. 'Don't worry if you see strange things in the night. He won't harm you.'

I never saw her husband, but Paddy was a constant visitor, and sometimes he would bring friends with him.

It was not long before the landlady said there were too many gentlemen visitors and she didn't like it. My conduct was unacceptable in a respectable house, she said. The sour looks of the Holy Mary statues hanging from the walls seemed to agree with her. Reluctantly, I had to return to the family home.

I got two surprises that Christmas. The first was a watch from Paddy. He said that when you wanted to marry a girl you gave her a watch first and then the ring came later. He didn't exactly ask me to marry him, he just wondered if I would like to be buried with his people. An Irish marriage proposal.

The second surprise was not so welcome. My period hadn't arrived and I was worried that I was pregnant. Paddy's preferred form of contraception was picked up in his native Ireland where, in the absence of anything else, coitus interruptus was used. Unfortunately, there was more coitus than interruptus going on in our sexual relations.

I told my parents that Paddy and I were thinking of getting married.

'You can't do that,' my father said, 'we hardly know him.'

'Wait a while,' my mother said, 'it's much too soon.'

It was clear to me that nobody in the family thought Paddy was good enough for me, and I couldn't understand why because as far as I could see our family was nothing special.

I knew what they were thinking. My father didn't want to see his Baby Ann wasting her life with this wild Irish boy. He thought I was meant for better things; after all, wasn't I going to college to learn how to be a teacher?

Paddy had, in his own way, already asked me to marry him, but neither of us was prepared for matrimony and a baby. We had only known one another a few months. I was looking forward to going to Leeds to train to be a teacher and we had talked about Paddy coming with me. But it was all different now. I couldn't be a student and mind a baby. Paddy was working as a labourer in the West End of London at the time, demolishing buildings, and I was teaching in Pitman's College and loving it.

I confided in my mother, who told my brother Ron. Together they decided that having a baby was out of the question. Besides, they said, it would kill my father if he knew I had got myself into trouble. That's what they called it then. Being pregnant outside of marriage was 'trouble' and that sounded about right to me at the time.

They decided that the obvious solution was for me to have an abortion. They came to that decision so easily and emphatically, even though abortion was illegal at that time in the UK. It didn't occur to me to wonder how they knew how to arrange such a thing. Many years later, my mother confessed to me that in between the birth of my sister and me, she had had an abortion herself.

My brother drove me in his car to an ordinary house, a few miles from my home, and waited outside. I knocked on the door and was greeted by a middle-aged woman in a paisley apron. The room was much the same as our own front room at home. The woman told me to take off my skirt and knickers and to lie down on the couch. She explained that she was going to wash the baby away. *Baby, what baby?* I thought. To me, it was a random seed, an accident, a mistake, a night of lovemaking.

The woman proceeded to insert a tube, attached to a funnel, into my vagina, and I heard a whooshing sound and felt a horrible sensation inside me. I lay there for what seemed like an hour, trembling and frightened, until she said, 'You can get dressed now. It will all be over in a couple of days.' My legs shook as I left the house, got into the car and drove home with my brother.

A couple of days turned into a week and nothing happened. I was still pregnant. My mother said that it was best if I told my father straight away: 'He's going to find out anyway and you have to tell him now.'

No matter how much drink had been taken the night before, my father rose early for work. I never knew him to stay in bed beyond 6.30 a.m., and on waking the first thing he did was to make his coffee in the electric percolator, the one upmarket domestic appliance in our house. It only ever got used in the morning and my father seemed to be the only one who knew how it worked. He drank his coffee black and he needed it that morning.

I got up early so that I could talk to him alone. The

bitter smell of the coffee followed him as he walked into the room. He was surprised to see me sitting there in the chair facing him across the table. I didn't waste any time, I just came out with it. 'I'm pregnant,' I said. 'I'm going to have a baby.'

My father had never raised his voice to me. I could do no wrong. I was the apple of his eye, as they say. But now, he was shouting, he was roaring. He called Paddy terrible names. He cried, and through his tears he said he didn't want to see either of us ever again.

He put on his coat and left for work. My mother consoled me and said he would come round, and he did. By the following day he had calmed down, but insisted that marriage plans should be made immediately.

I never did get an engagement ring and we bought our wedding rings from a stall on Walthamstow High Street. Everything had to be arranged in a great hurry so that no one would know that I *had* to get married.

In a few short months I had come from being a carefree, albeit lovesick, young woman to someone who was condemned to follow the prevailing societal rules. I was made to conform. There was no choice. We had no choice.

milestones

My birthday is not something I celebrate religiously. But I am scrupulous about remembering the birthdays of my children, their partners, grandchildren and close friends. I have a box in which I store cards, writing paper, stamps and my good pen. When I am out and about, I buy random cards to ensure it is always well stocked. In Covid-19 lockdown times, I resorted to buying birthday cards online.

It does not bother me if my birthday comes and goes without anyone remembering. I have been known to forget it myself. And as for Mother's Day, I told my children from a very early age that Mother's Day was a made-up thing. 'That's an American invention. Nothing to do with us,' I insisted. 'Don't even think about it. I don't need boxes of chocolates or bunches of flowers.'

I wasn't making it up. I did really believe that and still do. Hallmark Cards and others make a great profit out of it every year. Good luck to them. But as well as my principles, there were financial considerations. I didn't want them to spend their hard-earned money on such a made-up event. Best ignore it, forget it, I preached.

The same goes for Mothering Sunday, which falls on the fourth Sunday in Lent. That one was made up by the Church. Originally, Mothering Sunday meant that people visited their mother church, the one in which they were baptized. Nothing to do with mothers at all. Latterly, it became a day when domestic servants were given time off to visit their mothers and other family members.[1]

The fact is, I really don't like being the centre of attention, not any more. As a child, I got a lot of that. There is a big gap between myself and my sister, Joyce. She was eleven years old when I came along, while brothers Ron and Eddie were thirteen and sixteen.

From the very beginning, Baby Ann was loved and minded by everyone, especially my father. He called me Baby Ann until I was eight years old, when my mother made him stop.

I was born on 23 August 1939 in the German Hospital in the East End of London, eleven days before the Second World War began. My son Peter, who lives in London, sent me a photo recently of a plaque in commemoration of the German Hospital, in Dalston Lane. It is a housing complex now.

When my mother went into labour, it was my eldest brother, Eddie, who accompanied her to the hospital on the no. 38 bus. The story goes that the nurse asked him if he was the father. He must have been a very mature-looking young man, and my mother, at the age of thirty-nine, an unlikely partner.

---

1. I am reminded, as I write, of Graham Swift's novella *Mothering Sunday*, set in March 1924. The book focuses on a single day, but cleverly spans a life of nearly one hundred years. A beautiful, romantic story.

My second name is Marguerite, after the German midwife who assisted in my delivery. Soon after I was born, news of the impending war saw the doctors and nurses leaving London to get back to Germany. One day they were respected medical professionals and the next potential spies.

I can remember only one of my birthdays during wartime and that's because I have told the story so many times to my children and my grandchildren. We had gone to Cornwall to stay with my great-aunt Em because, after a lull of nearly three years, the Luftwaffe started bombing London again in early 1944. The 'Baby Blitz' it was called. My mother made me a big sponge cake with cream and jam. As I was away from home, I didn't have any friends to share it with, so Mum suggested I take a piece to a neighbour. A big slice was duly cut and I carried it carefully to the nearby bungalow. As I walked, I could not resist poking my finger in the cream that oozed from its side. I lifted the creamy finger to my lips and, as I did so, a bee followed it into my mouth. The bee stung me and I dropped the plate and screamed.

I didn't tell anyone when I returned home to London for fear of ridicule but, these days, I tell the story over and over again for the benefit of my younger grandchildren. 'Tell us again, Nanny, about the bee and the cake,' they say.

After the war, there were birthday parties galore,

where Baby Ann was overindulged. In my teens, I rebelled. Everybody got the message and left me alone.

On my twenty-first birthday, having left my newfound love in Cornwall, I was not happy, although the hundred pounds my father gave me cheered me up. A hundred pounds was a small fortune then. It didn't last long. I bought a coat and shoes, and lent fifty pounds to a friend in need. I never got it back.

After that, the big birthdays came and went for five decades without any great attention being paid to them by me or anyone else.

By the time I was thirty, I had six of my eight children and was too busy to think about birthdays.

At forty, my life revolved around the children and making sure Peter took his tablets and was safe.

I spent my fiftieth birthday in Greece with none of my family present, thank goodness. I had bought a white dress in the local market for the occasion. It was only when I got back to Ireland and had access to a full-length mirror that I realized it was entirely see-through. I have a tendency to make mistakes like that. I spent a whole Christmas Day once wearing a nightie that someone gave me because I thought it was a dress.

My sixtieth came and went without fuss. Most of my children were away in different parts of the world and the day was just like any other.

So the birthdays passed by in a blur till I got to seventy.

It took till then to really get into celebrating and if it wasn't for my children I might not have bothered. That birthday was a complete surprise and what a production it was. I was instructed to be ready at 12.30. Outside the door was a horse and trap in which Róisín and some of the younger grandchildren were seated. My first thought was for the poor horse and the heavy load he was carrying. I got over that quickly enough as the little ones snuggled up to me.

The driver took us to the National Maternity Hospital in Holles Street, where all my children were born. Outside, Michael and his wife, Rukhsana, were holding a huge banner on which was painted 'Nine months you carried me. Thanks Mum' in full view of everyone. That's when I started to cry.

As we trotted on, the bearers of the banner followed on foot until we arrived at the canal, beside the statue of Patrick Kavanagh, where the carriage halted. My good friend Daragh Downes was there with his guitar performing 'Raglan Road'. At Grosvenor Square we stopped again for a rendition of 'Are Ye Right There, Michael', which was one of Peter's favourite Percy French songs. At a roundabout on Dartmouth Square, my eldest grandchild, Fionn, played the uilleann pipes.

When we arrived at Rachael and Paul's house in Mountpleasant Square, everyone was there waiting for me. There was a splendid lunch, wine, presents and cake.

Sarah wrote a 'few' verses that say it all. If I quoted

them in full, I needn't have bothered writing this book at all. Here is just one verse that, for future reference, includes the names of my children.

> In your beatnik youth, you met a
> man, the true love of your life,
> Peter wooed with song and dance
> and you became his wife.
> You shared life with him in Dublin
> and eight children came to be,
> Sarah, Eddie, Brian, Rachael, Peter,
> Róisín, Michael and Katie.

For my eightieth birthday, there were spreadsheets and, in the background, lots of heated discussion. Where would it be held? Could everyone be there in the middle of August?

I was consulted this time, months before the event, and they asked me who I would like to invite. When I presented my list, there was consternation. Someone was heard to say, 'We'd need Croke Park for that.' And they would have done as I asked – invited everybody – only I changed my mind.

On St Stephen's Day 2018, I was with my family at a gathering in Kells. My mobile phone rang and I went outside to take the call. It was bad news: my brother Ron had died at the age of ninety-two. The man who had stood by me all my life was gone. The big bossy brother who always knew what was best. What a curmudgeon he was, even before he got old. 'I don't want to hear any small talk,' he protested if I, or anyone else, went on for too long about something that didn't interest him. He loved me in his own inimitable way. My elder brother, Eddie, had died some years before, and now there was only Joyce and me remaining.

I returned to the party to tell everybody. I was overwhelmed with their sympathy and love, from the youngest to the eldest. It was then that, through my tears, I decided all I needed and wanted was my family at the party. In the midst of my grief I came to that decision because of those spontaneous waves of affection. 'I can meet up with my friends later,' I told them. And that is exactly what I did.

The venue chosen was the Airfield Estate in Dundrum. I love the Airfield Estate, which was left in trust to the people of Ireland by Letitia and Naomi Overend in 1974. It is a beautiful thirty-eight-acre working farm and an oasis of natural beauty.

I arrived at that beautifully decorated room to see every one of my family, all thirty-three of them, there to greet me, with Gilbert O'Sullivan singing 'Nothing Rhymed' in the background. All my favourite songs were playing on a loop as we sat down to eat.

There was food and, in between each course, songs, saxophones, tin whistles and party pieces of every kind were performed by the grandchildren. And there were speeches.

My son Eddie addressed his speech to the grandchildren in the room. He told them that they had the qualities of their grandmother in their genes. 'There are three things about her which you are stuck with: innovation, community spirit and hard work,' he said. He then proceeded to elaborate on each of my attributes. 'She is also very funny,' he added and my grandchildren roared their agreement.

I was extremely moved, and if it had been all that was said about me on that day, it was enough. He hadn't mentioned my disregard for money, which he reminds me about on many occasions, and for that I was grateful.

The smaller children were taken off for a tour of the farm and then videograms were shown. That's the modern equivalent of telegrams.

I sat in amazement watching that big screen. Old friends, family in England and the good and the great of Ireland had sent me video messages. Gilbert O'Sullivan sitting on a bench in the sunshine in Jersey wished me a happy birthday. Róisín had written a column about him years before and I sent it to him addressed to 'Gilbert O'Sullivan, Jersey'. When he performed at the National Concert Hall in 2019, we had the best of seats.

After the cake, I was presented with a book full of photographs and lovely messages. The whole extraordinary day was filmed by my eldest granddaughter, Bláithín. If I am feeling down, and that has happened quite a lot while in lockdown, I watch the videograms and pore over the book and smile.

I am so proud of my children's ability to orchestrate these occasions. Both those birthdays were a culmination of hard work, a great outpouring of love and, of course, spreadsheets. So, I give you these two birthday stories as templates for anyone wishing to celebrate a loved one's anniversary. The first is probably only suitable for the extroverts among you; the second, for the more sophisticated. I wholeheartedly recommend them both.

I had three separate meet-ups with my different groups of friends after that. I brought along my book and shared the story of the grand day out.

That eightieth birthday party made me think again about my attitude to these celebrations. Maybe it's because I'm getting old. But, really, who am I to deny my family the obvious pleasure they got by giving me the best day any mother could ask for? Can't wait for my ninetieth now.

My feelings about the Mother's Day carry-on remain unchanged.

eyes wide open

These days, couples live together without marrying and think nothing of it. I have a daughter like that. In my day it was only bohemians, actresses and the arty crowd who dared to 'live in sin'. Back in 1961, as a fallen woman, I had little choice. I had to get married. Everyone said so.

I didn't care where we married, the venue wasn't important to me. Paddy insisted that we should marry in a Catholic church. I had never known him to show any interest in religious observance so I was confused. It appeared that you could take the man out of Catholic Ireland but the indoctrination lived on.

The nearest Catholic church was St Joseph's in Leytonstone. I telephoned to fix a date for the wedding, but the priest said we had to go in person to make the arrangements. 'Formalities must be observed,' he said.

When we arrived at the church, the priest brought us into a large room. It was sparsely furnished, cold and uninviting. I could see my face in the polished mahogany table where we were told to sit. Paddy and I sat on one side, the priest on the other. The room was clinically clean, but there was a strange smell in the air. It reminded me of my mother's potpourri that she kept on her dressing table.

I was nervous, naturally enough, having never been interviewed by a Catholic priest before, coupled with the fact that I had a secret. Well, I thought it was a secret, but I'm sure the priest must have known my dilemma. We were in a hurry. He had seen it all before.

Paddy had sent home for his baptismal certificate

and he handed it over with confidence. When the priest asked for mine, I gave him my birth certificate and told him I was christened in the Church of England.

'This complicates matters,' he said. 'You will have to obtain the permission of the bishop before the marriage can take place.'

The bishop, I thought, *what business is it of his?* The priest said, as if he were doing us a great favour, that he would approach this bishop and get back to us as soon as he could. As we got up to leave, he asked me if I realized that if we had children they would have to be brought up as Catholics. Furthermore, he told me, the ceremony could not take place before the main altar because I was not a Catholic.

So what, I thought, *any altar will do.* I wasn't thinking too deeply about bringing up my children with any religion at all. I couldn't imagine that a church would have the right to tell me that my children had to be Catholics.

The priest's words of warning fell on my ignorant ears. I knew nothing about Catholicism. I had gone to the local Church of England Sunday school as a child, and in my early teens I was fascinated by the idea of religion, always searching for something to belong to. Valerie, one of my friends at school, attended the local Baptist church. When Billy Graham, an evangelist from America, held a crusade in Harringay Arena, she brought me along. There were thousands in attendance that night and Billy Graham was a charismatic and persuasive speaker. I was spellbound, mesmerized. I wanted to give my life to Christ and I very nearly followed the crowds walking up to the stage as he beckoned them forward. Something held me back, probably the fact that I wasn't a hundred per cent sure there even was a God. But how that man could talk, what a salesman.

This priest wasn't trying to sell me anything. He didn't have the time nor the inclination to convert me. I was completely naive and unwittingly marrying into a Church that did not condone divorce, contraception or homosexuality, and barely tolerated mixed marriages. I recently came across an article written in 1906 in the *British Weekly* about the Irish, where the editor wrote:

> The priests control not only the worship but the life of the people. If the Irish peasant desires freedom he emigrates to America. I am told that not only peasants but even priests frequently cross the Atlantic, not for economic or worldly reasons at all, but to escape from the rigid and perfected system of the Roman obedience, which is, as Catholics think, the supreme blessing, and, as Protestants think, the most crushing bane of that lovely and melancholy land.

After several anxious phone calls to the priest, we were told that the bishop had given his consent. Once more, we sat at that table and the priest, pen in hand, started to fill in the necessary forms.

'What is your name?' he asked Paddy.

'Peter Ingle,' he replied.

I turned to him in confusion.

'What are you saying? Your name is Patrick Byrne,' I said, ignoring the kicks under the table that he was aiming at my legs. 'I've been calling you Paddy since we first met and now you say your name is Peter.'

Peter whispered that he would tell me about it later.

The priest looked from one to the other of us and shook his head.

'What year were you born?' came the next question.

'First of May 1939,' Peter replied.

'I was born in 1939,' I said, 'and you're three years older than me. You were born in 1936.'

'No, that's when Paddy Byrne was born,' Peter replied.

This was all too much for the priest. He rose and declared that this deceitful behaviour was no basis for a sacred union. In normal circumstances, he said, one meeting would have been sufficient. 'You'll have to sort this out between yourselves and come back to see me again next week,' he said as he escorted us out.

Before we left, he gave us some leaflets to read, one of which was written by John C. Heenan, Archbishop of Liverpool, and stated:

A marriage is not something you can try to see how it will turn out. Once you marry there is no going back. You may discover in later years that you have made an unwise choice. Your partner may prove unkind or unfaithful. War, sickness, loss of a job, crime, anything may spoil the ideal marriage you had imagined. But if you are married nothing will break the marriage bond. There will be no question of divorce. That is one reason why it is so important for you to go into marriage with a Catholic with your eyes wide open.

Eyes wide open! I thought they were up until then. But . . . Peter? My husband-to-be was Peter, not Paddy. Peter.

Peter insisted it was all very straightforward and couldn't understand what I was so upset about. He explained that when he first came to England he had taken the identity of a neighbour from Dublin, Paddy Byrne, because he was too young to work in the brewery in Sheffield where a friend had got him a job. He said he didn't think it was important so he had never bothered to tell me.

'What difference does it make?' he said. 'Everyone calls me Paddy over here.' That was true – everyone with an Irish accent was a Paddy.

We went back to St Joseph's the next week and this time the priest gave us a solemn sermon about the sanctity of marriage and the implications of being married to someone of a different faith. But despite his lecture and obvious misgivings, he agreed to marry us. Just like my father, the priest knew what had to be done.

*

My ignorance was abysmal, and not only about bishops and the Catholic Church. There were probably many women like me who did not realize that after marriage they were the property of their husband and he could use them in any way he wanted, no matter what their religion. The principle was established by St Augustine and brought into law by Sir Matthew Hale in 1736 when he wrote: 'But the husband cannot be guilty of rape committed by himself upon his lawful wife, for by their mutual matrimonial consent and contract, the wife hath given herself up in this kind unto her husband which she cannot retract.' It wasn't until 1991 that this law was changed in the UK and in Ireland at around the same time.

There was so much I didn't know – about everything, but especially about Peter. Not knowing his name and age was a big one. And I hadn't even met his parents or brothers and sisters, all thirteen of them.

During those few weeks before the wedding, Peter was not his usual easy-going self. He felt he was being rushed into things. And he was, but so was I. I would have been happy to carry on the way we were and see what happened.

A week before the wedding, Peter met an old friend from Ireland, who he invited to the ceremony. The night before the big day, they went out together on an impromptu stag night. Peter was staying with Ron, who rang me at midnight to tell me Peter wasn't home yet. I knew that if Peter disappeared, nobody would mind, and I sensed that in my brother's voice. He was preparing me for the worst.

I was confident and remained calm. I knew that nothing would stop our wedding and I laughed at my brother for thinking otherwise. 'Don't worry,' I said, knowing full well that he wasn't a bit worried. 'He'll turn up.' And he did.

On 11 February 1961, seven months after we had first set eyes on one another, Peter and I were married. My niece was the bridesmaid and we both wore hired outfits, which went back the next day. The service was over in minutes. After seeing many weddings in Catholic churches in the years that followed, I realized that ours had been a half-hearted affair. A ceremony specially designed for a hasty mixed marriage.

There was a cold buffet, sparkling wine and a barrel of beer back in Ron's house. He had arranged a few days' honeymoon for us in Oxford. We climbed the Saxon Tower, walked around the quadrangles of Christ Church College and hired a punt. As Peter propelled us along the River Cherwell, I lay back, imagining myself a student there.

After that brief holiday, our married life began living with Ron and his wife, Eva, in their house in Southgate while we were looking for a flat to rent.

It was a few weeks later when I started to haemorrhage. I lay in bed that night in great pain, bleeding heavily. Why I wasn't sent straight to the hospital, please don't ask me. It could be the British stiff upper lip, or not wanting to bother the doctor in the middle of the night, or more likely the fear that it would be found out that I had attempted to have an abortion. Lots of towels were handed into the bedroom with a few aspirins as Peter lay beside me in the bed trying to comfort me and ease my pain. When the doctor was eventually sent for in the morning, he immediately organized an ambulance and I spent the next two days in hospital.

I had grown used to the idea of being a mother and, despite everything, was looking forward to having a baby. And now the reason we had married in haste was gone and I worried I was going to lose Peter too. I was waiting every minute for Peter to tell me that our marriage was a mistake.

One evening I came home from work to find Eva and Peter at the piano. She was accompanying him as he sang 'You'll Never Know (Just How Much I Love You)'. When I came into the room, Peter walked over to me, still singing, and as he took me in his arms, I felt at that moment there was, maybe, a chance of happiness for the two of us.

If Peter and I were going to make a life together, we needed time to adjust to one another on our own. We found ourselves a flat, moved out of my brother's house, and my life as a married woman began.

milkman

In the 1960s, everyone relied on milk being delivered to their doorsteps in foil-topped bottles each morning. The milkman arrived early in his white electric float and clanked his way up the garden path to leave the day's supply. If you ordered a pint of Jersey milk, there would be at least an inch of cream at the top. Gorgeous in a cup of coffee.

Our Express Dairies milkman called with the bill at the end of the week. The trouble was we always seemed to miss him. So, after a few weeks when the bill wasn't paid, he stopped delivering. That meant we had to remember to buy milk from the shop. Neither of us liked black tea. At least we had that in common.

As we started out on our married life, I found that Peter and I were very different in many ways. He liked to stay up late. He would sit beside the record player for hours until he had the words of the songs off by heart, whereas I was an early-to-bed person.

Peter's musical taste was eclectic and he might as easily be listening to Nat King Cole singing jazz as to tenors like Brendan O'Dowda singing Percy French, or Richard Tauber singing arias, or songs from Franz Lehár operettas. I loved those Lehár songs, especially 'Girls Were Made to Love and Kiss' and, best of all, 'You Are My Heart's Delight'.

> You are my heart's delight,
> And where you are, I long to be

You make my darkness bright,
When like a star you shine on me
Shine, then, my whole life through
Your life divine bids me hope anew
That dreams of mine may at last come true
And I shall hear you whisper, 'I love you'.

I am listening to that song as I write and thinking of some of the happy times we had in that flat as we were learning about one another. But I have to be realistic and remember that the year we spent there was not all heart's delight and life divine.

I loved playing house in our little flat. I cooked and cleaned and made like the good wife. That was just what women did in those days and it was a pattern that was set for the rest of my married life.

I went to a family planning clinic and was fitted with a diaphragm, which was about the only way a woman could prevent an unwanted pregnancy in the early 1960s. It's little used now, but back then a diaphragm was the commonest form of contraception for women – it was a small, soft, rubber dome, about seven centimetres in diameter, that you would squeeze at the rim to make it into a narrow oval shape for insertion into the vagina to cover the cervix. It had to be put in before intercourse and kept in place for at least six hours afterwards. Then you took it out and washed it, and you could use it again as soon as you wanted. (Of course, after childbirth, your body changes so you needed to be fitted with a new one. By the time I had my first baby I was in Ireland and there was no hope of popping along to the doctor to get that sorted. So that was the end of the diaphragm.)

We both went back to work. We got on with life, but for Peter it wasn't so easy. He couldn't get his head around the fact that he was no longer single. He wasn't prepared to play the game, like me. If it hadn't been for the milk, we might have carried on like that for years.

Peter was on his way home in the early hours of one Saturday morning when he stole a bottle of milk from a random doorstep. A very alert and zealous policeman on night duty saw him and Peter was arrested. In the police station he tried to escape out of the window, like a cowboy in a western. He was 'vigorously restrained' as they say in newspaper reports when people are manhandled. This was the era of 'no Irish, no blacks, no dogs', and Peter's accent was pure Irish.

On that Saturday morning, a policeman arrived at the door with the news. He told me that Peter had been apprehended stealing milk and that he was in the police station in Luton, miles away.

'For stealing a bottle of milk?' I said.

The policeman explained that Peter had previous convictions in Bedfordshire.

At the police station, the first officer I met treated me with contempt and acted as if I were somehow responsible for Peter's actions. He took delight in telling me that Peter had assaulted a man in High Wycombe three years back.

'He was granted bail but he didn't turn up for the next court appearance,' the officer said.

I could handle that, just about, but the officer went on to say that Peter had had sex with an underage girl and left her pregnant.

I sat there, stunned. 'You've made a mistake,' I said. 'That can't be right.'

The policeman shrugged and said, 'Ask him yourself.'

When I went into the cell, Peter had a cut lip and a black eye, and his clothes were torn and dirty.

'Is that man telling the truth?' I asked. 'Tell me it's all a big mix-up.'

But he couldn't, it wasn't. It was true.

Peter had been in a fight and had been charged with assault. He was granted bail but decided it was best to move on before the case came to court.

As for the girl, Peter told me that he hadn't known how old she was and assumed that she was eighteen, the same age as himself. 'How was I to know?' he said.

I looked at him sitting there in that cell. Who was this man? I felt I didn't know him at all.

'Help me,' he said.

On the bus journey back to London, I was confused and bewildered.

I went to my parents, they would know what to do. My mum and dad were busy when I got there. Their boxer dog had just had pups. Those newborn puppies created a diversion for a while until eventually they stopped fussing over the dogs and looked at my face, puffy and red from crying.

Through my tears, I told them the awful story. I told them about the policeman and how Peter had been beaten up. I told them it wasn't his fault, although I hardly believed that myself. They were furious, not only with him but also with me for some reason. First, I had felt the policeman was blaming me and now my own parents. I hated their 'we told you so' faces. I couldn't bring myself to tell them about the girl and the baby. I was having a hard enough time trying to come to terms with it myself.

Brother Ron came to the rescue again and we talked to a solicitor. Peter appeared in Luton Crown Court a few days later. He was refused bail because of his having absconded previously. I had never been in a courtroom before and, as I watched Peter in the dock, it felt unreal, like a play. Peter was put on remand in Bedford Prison for two months to await trial.

My brother and parents were muttering things about divorce and being married under false pretences. I didn't feel like that at all. I wanted to help him get through this although I hated the thought of the girl and the child.

I wrote to him and visited as often as I could, and he wrote back.

Here is a love letter, the first he ever sent me. It was written on skimpy prison notepaper.

Bedford Prison
Inmate number 2888
June 28, 1961

Dear Ann

The first thing that I would like to tell you is that I love you with all my heart and everything that is part of me Ann, darling. I don't think that I ever called you darling before because I just could not say something I did not mean. When I say a beautiful thing like that to you it is because you are a darling and the most beautiful girl and wife in this whole world and I love you more than anything material or otherwise that is in it, my precious thing. You are the most delightful, most fabulous, most fantastic creature that was born of this earth and how I got you I just don't know.

The first time we met you cast a spell on me although you did not know it. I began to think that you were a witch and I said to myself why haven't I met this witch before now and myself said to I: you would never have appreciated her or the charm divine that she has got. This girl, woman of so many talents and my wife I love you Ann dearest because well let me explore it. It's very hard for me to explain in conversation so I will write the reasons. You, Ann dearest are the most understanding, patient and most truthful woman there is alive today. Also you have the most beautiful body a woman could hope to ask or even hope for. Because you are the most desirable, womanly and most feminine wife any man on this earth would ever ask for when he is looking for someone to spend the rest of his life with.

My heart cries for you Ann my dearest Ann. I miss you so much more than I ever could have imagined. Just to see you smile again happily is what I want to see. For us to laugh together and go swimming and do the things that make life worthwhile. I keep on telling you how much I love you but do you still love me the way you say you do? I will close now Ann dearest not much more room left. So goodbye and God bless.

From your ever loving husband

Peter

As I sit with that letter in my hand today, I am once again overcome. He did love me, he really did, just as much as I loved him. The magic of our first meeting was not my imagination, it was real.

Oh, how I loved his letters. It was a revelation to me that Peter could compose such a beautifully worded message. He had left school at fourteen and I'd had no idea that he could write like that. I delighted in every loving word.

At Peter's trial, the girl dropped the charge against him. She had since married and moved on, and wanted nothing more to do with Peter. She was there in the court holding the hand of a beautiful, blond, curly-haired child who looked like a miniature version of my husband. And that was the last we saw of the boy.

Peter was fined for the fight with the man in High Wycombe and the judge was lenient because no weapons had been used, apart from Peter's fists. Peter's eldest brother, James, came to the court so at least now I knew one of Peter's family.

The fine was paid, and Peter and I came home to our flat together. Things changed. Peter was more affectionate and loving than ever and I was happy.

A few weeks after he came out of prison, Peter showed me a letter. He said there would be no more secrets between us. I thought by now I knew everything but I was mistaken. As I read the letter, I felt a chill come over me. Would there be no end to this?

The letter was dated 27 December 1959, six months before I met him. It was from a girl called Pat.

Dear Pete [at least he must have given her his real name]

Just a few lines to thank you very much for the money you sent Julie for Christmas and I would like to thank you also for the dress you sent her a few weeks ago. I would have written and thanked you before but you know what I am, I kept putting it off and saying I'll get some writing paper today but I never did. But today I finally got some. As you can see, Julie is fine and she's coming on smashing. She's just like a big fat dumpling and the image of you. She's got your eyes and nose, her hair only curls when I've washed it. I hope she has curly hair. At the moment she is fast asleep. She isn't a bit of trouble at all and she is cutting her teeth, two front ones.

I hope you've had a happy Christmas Pete. It's not been bad for me. The only trouble is I won't leave Julie yet. She's too young so Christmas for me is just like any other day, means staying in. But it won't always be like this.

So I'll close now Pete and all the best for the coming year.

Yours truly
Pat

PS I'm sorry it had to be the way it was when you came up Pete. But we wasn't meant for each other.

Pat and Peter were not 'meant for each other'. I didn't ask him if he had bought her a watch too, but I thought about it. They were only seventeen years old when that baby was conceived. It unsettled me. Here was a woman with a baby and yet she could let him go. She didn't fall under his spell. I wondered how many more children with blond curly hair had been born since Peter left Ireland. And, bizarrely, I was jealous. He must have loved her and the baby, and how many others, I wondered.

This letter was now another secret we shared. I wasn't about to tell anyone, least of all my family. I knew how they would react so I was on my own with this one too.

We talked about it and decided to send Pat some

money. There was no reply, and Peter said she must have moved on and that was that. I tried not to think any more about it, but Peter sometimes mentioned Julie, wondering where or how she was.[1]

At this point, I could have gone. I could have done what my family recommended and left him. But I didn't.

We found a new milkman. We changed to London Co-op Dairies and carried on, for better or for worse.

---

1. After Peter's death, when my children were old enough, I told them about Julie and the other child. I thought they should know. To my knowledge, they have not looked for their half-siblings.

tomorrow's world

I learned to type on a typewriter that had no letters or numbers on the keyboard. As we practised, the teacher put on a gramophone record and we typed to the rhythm of the music. It was quaint. Twenty fourteen-year-old girls typing away blindly to the sound of a brass band.

It was before photocopiers were invented, so to produce multiple copies you had to use a Gestetner machine. We had one in our school. You inserted a sheet of wax-coated paper into the typewriter and, as you typed, impressions were made in the wax of the letters, punctuation and other marks. You then took this sheet to the Gestetner machine, set it up on a revolving drum, turned the handle and, after a lot of whirring and clunking, duplicates emerged.

I left secretarial college at sixteen and went to work in the Extramural Department of the University of London as secretary to one of the lecturers. Mr Burrows was a great mentor and introduced me to Arnold Bennett, Émile Zola and Bach. He said I was 'too old for toys and too young for boys'. I took letters and reports down in shorthand and then went back into the open-plan office, where four other girls were clattering away on their typewriters.

Accuracy was all-important in those days, as mistakes had to be rectified using a hard rubber eraser. This became even more difficult and time-consuming if you were using carbon paper to make copies. A correction fluid, Tipp-Ex, came into vogue in the late 1950s but was messy to use and not much help with the carbon copies. All this was still before photocopiers, or Xerox machines, as they were originally called. It is impossible for younger generations to imagine how laborious it was in my day.

I never stopped typing. I worked from home, creating my own little cottage industry. It was one of my main sources of income for many years, along with the Children's Allowance and, after Peter died, the Widow's Pension. I became well known for it. If anyone needed a letter or a school project typed, they knew where to go. Many people, far outside my social circle, came knocking. How else would I have met Michael Morris, 3rd Baron Killanin, President of the International Olympic Committee, an MBE, journalist and author?

For several months I typed Lord Killanin's memoir, transcribing the tapes from the Dictaphone he supplied. He spoke so beautifully with his posh English accent, I loved listening to him. He lived in a big house on Lansdowne Road and arrived at my door on a bicycle, with clips around his trouser legs and his grey hair all awry. The book, *My Olympic Years*, was published in 1983.

Mary Lavin, the short-story writer and novelist, was another client. Mary was the mother of Valdi Mac Mahon, and grandmother to author Kathleen Mac Mahon, who was only a child then. The Mac Mahons lived opposite us in a house called Castleville on the Green. Mary had come to live in Sandymount and was still writing and editing her work, and Valdi recommended me.

Mary would talk for ages as I sat captivated, not daring to interrupt. She was that kind of woman. You wouldn't think of stopping her when she was in full flow. I can see her now, with her abundance of grey hair, her black dress always adorned with silver jewellery, as she handed me sheaves of handwritten pages to type. Mary was a demanding woman, although always very nice to me. I seem to remember she complained a lot about her publisher.

I was honoured and a little dazzled when the writer Frank McGuinness arrived on my doorstep one morning with his gorgeous smile and a manuscript for me to type. What a generous, lovely man he is. We still exchange Christmas cards.

I also worked for the late actress and singer Agnes Bernelle when she was writing her autobiography *The Fun Palace*. Later, her son, Seán, who wrote science fiction, and her daughter, Antonia, joined my list of favourite clients.

I sometimes ventured outside of the house to work for the McKennas, local solicitors, and Finnegan Menton, estate agents, on Sandymount Green.

I particularly remember one of the temp jobs I had with James Adams and Sons, Fine Art Auctioneers and Valuers on St Stephen's Green. I was shown to my desk and given a document to type, and I was ready to make a good impression. The keys of the typewriter would not move. I poked and prodded but they would not respond to my touch. I tried to catch someone's eye, but at the same time I was reluctant to expose my ignorance. I eventually realized there was a wire attached to the machine, found the switch and away I went. It was the first electric typewriter I had encountered.

I was secure and confident in my ability to earn money as a typist until the evening when the twins called me from the kitchen to look at the television. They were watching *Tomorrow's World*. There before me on the screen was a young woman typing at a computer, demonstrating how to miraculously move text around and delete it at the tap of a key. She showed how text could be placed on a floppy disk (which wasn't floppy at all but a 3.5-inch square in a rigid casing) and taken to another computer. It dawned on me that in the not too distant future my trusty typewriter would be a collector's item.

Some time later, Anne O'Rourke, a neighbour, suggested I took a course in word processing. A relation of hers was teaching a full-time course in Word Processing and Modern Office Procedures in AnCO[1]. In 1986, I enrolled on that course to begin my entry into the modern world. My fast typing and unbounded enthusiasm

---

1. An acronym for the state training agency, An Chomhairle Oiliúna. AnCO was succeeded by FÁS, which in turn became SOLAS – also acronyms for their official Irish language names.

saw me leaving the course three months later with a piece of paper saying I was trainee of the year.[2]

A local company, Microdot, had just opened on Sandymount Green and I went to work with Dot Fisher, the owner, who became a lifelong friend. We provided our services to businesspeople, students, solicitors and a junior barrister who is now a Supreme Court judge. Dot arranged for us both to qualify as teachers and we went on to instruct others in the wondrous art of word processing.

I was on top of my game, or so I thought, but things change. It came home to me the summer I worked as a temp at a big accountancy firm, Stokes Kennedy Crowley. I was assigned the job of typing a special report on RTÉ. The man in charge watched me working; in fact, he looked over my shoulder far too much for my liking – he was getting free lessons on how to manage the computer that had just been assigned to him. And that's how it started – personal computing.

Do I sound disgruntled? Well, I was at the time. The

---

2. You will have gathered by now that my children are exceptional people. I managed to do the course because my older children undertook to cook the dinner every evening and look after the younger ones. They were given five pounds per day to purchase what they needed and turn it into a meal for nine. Eddie went a bit cordon bleu and used every pot in the house.

world and her husband are typing away on laptops now and a lot of them have even learned to touch type.

I bought a new laptop last month because the old one was beginning to purr at me and I was worried it would collapse. I have worked my way through many types of software and now I am on to Microsoft Word 365. This was a little challenging at first because it looked a bit different on the screen but basically the functions are the same. I now have OneDrive, which is a great innovation. Not having to back everything up or send text to myself on an email in case it is lost is a great advantage. The idea of everything I write being 'up in the cloud' appeals to me. My words floating around with Anne Enright's and all those other literary giants excites me. Only, what Microsoft decided to do with the spellcheck is outrageous. It is small and situated over to one side, especially annoying for someone like me with macular degeneration. I know others, not just old ones like me, who find it difficult to cope with upgrades. I heard Lee Child, the detective fiction writer, on the radio the other day. He had the new version of Word and was not a bit happy. Apparently, Mr Child has a problem with headers and confessed that instead of starting a new document, he simply deletes the last novel and uses that empty document for his template.

With a good broadband connection, I can google away to my heart's content. No encyclopedias needed to find out which female tennis player won the most Grand Slams (Serena Williams with a total of twenty-three) or which is the highest mountain in Ireland (Carrauntoohil, of course). I don't have to consult Britannica any more. In any case, I couldn't read the print with my wonky eyes. I have a huge television screen I use for my monitor, so no problems there.

I am grateful to be able to read my newspapers of choice, the *Guardian* and the *Irish Times*, online. I use email, Twitter, Facebook, Instagram and WhatsApp. During Covid-19 times, I acquired a camera for Zoom. Being able to communicate with friends and family by email is wonderful, although there is nothing quite like getting a letter in the post, as I did this morning from my daughter-in-law Katy in North Carolina.

Because of FÁS[3] regulations, I was forced to retire from my job as Supervisor for Sandymount Community Services when I reached the age of sixty-six, after working there for three years. I needed a project and started a blog on WordPress called 'After Retirement'. After about a year or so I stopped as hardly anyone was reading it and it was like talking to myself. You can go mad that way. It is still there if you want to look at it. I remember I posted some lovely pictures of Katie's wedding, and

---

3. An acronym for the state training agency, An Foras Áiseanna Saothair (the Training and Employment Authority), the successor to AnCO.

after mentioning colonic irrigation one week, I got a lot more readers, but that was only temporary.

On the strength of writing a whole load of nonsense on that blog, I was nominated for a Silver Surfer Award. I received a runner-up certificate, which was presented to me by the late broadcaster Derek Davis, such a lovely man. He was impressed that I was the mother of Róisín Ingle, for which I got an extra round of applause.

I am proud that I joined Twitter long before my journalist daughter, who is now an avid user both for work and socially. I don't post very much, but I like to make a comment here and there, and often refer people to articles I have read in the newspapers. You can only use 280 characters per tweet. Instead of waffling, tweeters must come straight to the point. But it can be a terrible time-waster if you don't take yourself in hand.

I asked my housemates if they thought I should explain here how each social media platform works. *No*, they said, *anyone reading your book will know all that*, but I'm not sure. I have a son who rarely uses social media. I find his constant cry of 'I don't even know what a hashtag is' most annoying. I tell him a # in front of a word or phrase draws attention to something, and people connect and comment – #keepupson.

Yesterday, one of my daughters asked me why a photograph of me sitting outside my house with a mask on had appeared on WhatsApp.

'That wasn't me,' I told her. 'That was a meme of Bernie Sanders.'

'A what?' she said.

I use Facebook less frequently. My grandchildren say it is only for old people. Well, that includes me but, somehow, I never really got into it.

Instagram is for me the darling of all social media platforms. Apart from family and friends, I also follow people I admire or want to know more about: Kevin Dundon (of the best brown bread recipe in the world), Nigella Lawson, Jack Monroe and Nadiya Hussain for the cooking, Niall Breslin for the mind, and loads more.

It's great to have all these virtual friends, but the dark side of social media brings me to tears. There are some very nasty people out there who thrive on trying to ruin people's reputations and lives with their negativity. What did the performer Maureen Potter say at the end of her shows? 'If you liked the show, tell your friends, and if you didn't, keep your breath to cool your porridge.'

I have had a smartphone for a long time now. Of course, it took a little while to master all the intricacies and still I don't know it all. But when I go for a walk, I am rewarded with a message telling me how many steps I have taken. I get reminded to take my calcium tablets twice a day. I can access my emails and Instagram, listen to my audiobooks through my Bluetooth headphones and use WhatsApp while I am out and about. Not so much of that during these months of Covid but it will come again, it will.

Of course, I am not totally au fait with all the latest applications available. My grandchildren use Snapchat, TikTok and Discord. Video gaming is extremely popular with the young ones too, but my only competitive sport these days is a game of Hearts.

My favourite gadget is my Google Home. Peter and Aoife, my son and daughter-in-law, bought it for me a few Christmases ago and now I couldn't live without it. I've just asked it to play 'In Waiting' by Pillow Queens, because someone I know mentioned it on Twitter. I'll check it out before I ask Google to go back to the brilliant Jack L.

When I wake up, I say, 'Hey, Google. Good morning.'

'Good morning, Ann,' she says politely and then goes on to tell me the date and the weather, and connects me to the latest news. I can ask her to play any radio station, any podcast and any song that comes into my head. She helps me with the crossword too. The only thing she can't do is make me a cup of tea. If I were the head of looking after older people in Ireland, I would ensure that everyone over seventy had one free of charge.

The old typewriter was a beautiful machine, and in some ways I was sorry to say goodbye to it. But, now, my laptop and Google are my new BFFs[4].

---

4. That's 'best friends forever'.

madly, deeply

At the end of our first traumatic married year, Peter and I were closer than ever. He was kind and tender and grateful for my love and forgiveness. We were, as the cliché goes, madly in love. In love, madly.

We went to Ireland for Christmas. I wanted to know about the family I had married into; he was just pining for home.

Our BEA flight landed in Aerfort Bhaile Átha Cliath on that cold December morning in 1961. The first thing that struck me was how beautiful the terminal building was and the second was that I couldn't understand a word anyone was saying. I assumed they were speaking Irish, but Peter insisted they were speaking in English. I had got used to Peter's way of talking, calling the sink a 'trow' and the cupboard a 'press', and other strange things, but this was not just the words – this was a whole language which I could not recognize as English.

Peter had got excited when he saw the two big red-and-white-striped chimneys looming towards us as we neared the airport and he pointed out the little island, Ireland's Eye. Our flight had arrived in the early hours of the morning and, not wanting to wake everyone too early, Peter brought me first to O'Connell Street. He wanted to show me Nelson's Pillar.[1] *The last time I looked*, I thought, *he was in Trafalgar Square.*

---

1. The Irish Nelson's Pillar was built in 1809. It stood in the middle of O'Connell Street for 157 years until 8 March 1966

'It's only sixpence to go up inside it, a hundred and sixty-six steps,' he said. 'It was built from granite brought here from the Wicklow Mountains.'

He showed me McDowells, the Happy Ring House. 'We can buy your engagement ring there,' he said.

'I don't need that any more, Peter,' I said, 'we're married now.'

We got the bus to Margaret Place, the family home. It was one thing not being able to communicate with baggage handlers and ticket officials but when I heard Peter's mother also speaking in what seemed to my ears a foreign language, I felt like turning around and going back to London.

Mrs Ingle – Sarah – had not been at our wedding and, despite the fact that I showed her the photographs of Peter and me outside St Joseph's with family and friends in attendance, I don't think she really believed that we were married. Maybe she just didn't like the idea of her son sleeping with a Protestant. I don't know. In any case, on that first night I was told I would be sleeping in a room with Peter's youngest brother, Tony. Strangely, this seemed perfectly acceptable to Mrs Ingle, but Peter was furious that she would even suggest it.

A bed was made up for us in what was called 'the loft',

---

when it was destroyed by Republicans who, unlike me, were experts in Ireland's past and did not agree with Nelson taking pride of place in Dublin's central thoroughfare.

although it was to the side of the house. This 'loft' had been converted to a gym for the Ingle boys to train in so I spent my first night in Ireland with a punchball hanging from the ceiling over my head.

Mrs Ingle proudly told me that she had fifteen children and rattled off their names: James, John, Charles, Marcella, Rose, Michael Joseph, Christopher, Ignatius, Bernard, Edmund, Bridget, Patricia, Peter, Brendan and Anthony, counting them on her fingers as she spoke. They were all good saints' names as was the Catholic tradition.

That Christmas, only Tony and Bridget were still living at home. The others were scattered over the world in New Zealand, Canada and England, while some remained in Dublin. Of the fifteen children, two had died. Rose had died at birth and Michael Joseph from a heart condition in his early twenties.

Peter had boasted of living in a castle and I knew that was only a fantasy, but his description of Dublin was just as he had told me – the beach, the sea and the mountains were all close by. He introduced me to his friends and they accepted me, although they did make fun of my English accent. I didn't mind too much.

No public houses are open in Ireland on Christmas Day so, after the Christmas dinner, Peter took me to find somewhere to have a drink. All you had to do was call at someone's house, where you would be sure of hospitality, if they weren't teetotallers like the Ingles, of course. I had discovered that when a huge Christmas pudding was produced by Peter's mother and I enquired if they were going to light it, as was customary in my own home, and was met with blank faces. They didn't have drink in the house so the spirit required to douse the pudding was not available. That was a big surprise as Peter loved a drink and going to the pub was one of his favourite leisure pursuits.

A nearby sports club, Railway Union, was another place to go if you knew the right people. We passed by a square surrounded by houses, which, despite the high railings and tall, menacing-looking trees, I was drawn to. It reminded me of one of those small squares that are often found in the centre of London. This was Sandy-mount Green. I had no inkling then, of course, that it would be my home for thirty-six years.

When we returned to London, Peter talked about how great it would be if we could live in Dublin. Peter loved swimming, walking and fishing. He loved the outdoor life almost as much as the inside of a public house. And there was little of the outdoor life to be had where we were living.

Dublin to me was more like a provincial town than a capital city, but I liked it. I liked the people too and the idea grew on me. London is great if you are young and single, but I wanted a family and Ireland seemed a good place for that.

The decision was made. We were both working full-time so we left our flat, moved in with my parents and saved every penny we could. For some of the time, Peter was working on a building site in Cumberland in the north of England and I was working in London. So more love letters were exchanged as well as long-distance telephone calls. Peter reversed the charges when he rang and my father did not appreciate it when the telephone bill arrived.

One of the reasons for the length of those calls was that Peter sang to me and I couldn't get enough of his version of a Frank Ifield number, 'I Remember You', that was popular at the time.

I remember you too, Peter. How could I ever forget?

We splashed out for one idyllic long weekend in Cornwall before the move. We fished for mackerel, swam naked in the sea and went back to the rented cottage to make love. I am looking now at the painting of Mevagissey we bought that weekend. We saw the artist at the harbour, painting, and Peter said we had to buy it. It was an extravagance – it cost eleven guineas – but I am so glad I have it.

Peter was always great like that. On the way to the pictures one afternoon, we passed a garage selling used cars. He spotted this huge old Austin car, complete with running board, and decided it would be just the thing to take us and our belongings to Ireland. I hadn't even known he could drive.

November 1962, we loaded that car with everything we owned. It was a marvel it reached Holyhead at all.

In those days, you couldn't drive on to the boat. We watched as the old car, suspended by ropes, swung high in the air before coming down with a bang on the deck.

We arrived in Dublin in great style in our Austin car.

Margaret Place, Bath Avenue, Dublin 4 was to be our home until we managed to find a house we could afford. Peter got work on the docks, loading and unloading the boats that came up the Liffey. I didn't bother to look for work because by that stage I was pregnant. I had discarded the diaphragm and we were both happy and ready to start a family in our own home. Some of the best times during this period were when Peter and I drove around in the old car looking at properties.

The baby was born in the National Maternity Hospital, Holles Street, on 21 July 1963. I called her Sarah but not because it was her grandmother's name. As a young girl I had always loved that name and said that if I had a girl when I got married I would call her Sarah. You know the way you do.

From then on Sarah accompanied us in our search for a home. One house in Greystones, with a stream running at the end of the garden, was idyllic, and I imagined myself living there with children and chickens. Only imagined, because I knew it wasn't feasible for me to suddenly become a countrywoman and for Peter to give up his local pub and everything that went with it.

We bought no. 8 Sandymount Green in August 1963

for 2,000 Irish pounds. It was over a hundred years old and needed a lot of work. We were warned that the house was damp and not a good buy, but we didn't listen. It was just around the corner from the Sandymount Strand, with the Green on the doorstep, and I loved it. Peter liked it just as much as I did, so we went ahead.

The house deal went through in October 1963 and the monthly repayments were eleven punts, twelve shillings and sixpence per month. A paltry amount by today's standards but, even so, it was a struggle sometimes to make that payment.

After paying the deposit on the house, we had nothing left. We rented out the house unfurnished and went back to London to live once again with my parents. Peter worked for my brother and I obtained a position as a shorthand typist with a company five minutes' walk from my parents' home.

My mother looked after Sarah while I was at work and I came home at lunchtime each day to feed her. She was very good to do this for me and I appreciated it. I helped with the housework and she did the cooking – her steamed suet puddings were the stuff of culinary dreams. She was a great seamstress and knitter, and I admired that about her. But really we were never that close. I think maybe my father's devotion to me got in the way of a proper mother/daughter relationship. She had to cope with my father's flirting, drinking and gambling, and, as a young woman, I found her nagging and arguing with him irritating. As my own marriage progressed, I began to understand her frustrations. Today, I look back at my mother's constant struggle with my father's indiscretions and wish I had been more sympathetic.

We left before the end of that year, having saved up what we considered a substantial sum of money. I left the house where I had grown up, never to return, as my parents were retiring to live in Cornwall later that year. I was going to miss them and they were sorry to see little Sarah go as they had become very attached to her. But we were moving once more – a young family ready to start the next adventure.

Arriving back in Dublin in October 1964 was a culture shock all over again. How could I have forgotten so quickly that croissants would not be on the menu in Sandymount, and I would have to go to Bewley's in the city centre to get a decent cup of coffee? Grafton Street wasn't that far, really – ten minutes on a bus, or you could even walk there in forty minutes – but that seemed a lot of effort just for a coffee.

We began renovations. Every time work was complete on one part of the house, we found some other fault that needed to be remedied. It was a never-ending job. Peter's friends helped out at first but as time went by everyone seemed to lose interest.

In the midst of all this chaos, nature took its course and I gave birth to twins, Eddie and Brian, on 8 March

1965. Peter was delighted that he had gained two sons in one go and celebrated with enthusiasm and several pints.

One would have thought that with three children under two, it was time to take precautions, but it wasn't that easy in holy Catholic Ireland. Call me irresponsible, but I loved Peter and our sexual relationship was very important to me. I have a friend who made a point of having a row with her husband just as they turned off the television for the night. That was her solution to the absence of any other kind of protection. I soon fell pregnant again and Rachael was born on 23 April 1966. At the age of twenty-six, I was the mother of four children under three: a newborn, one-year-old twins and a toddler.

In 1968, after a year of instruction, I became a Catholic. Peter was happy about it and should have been there beside me in the chapel when I made my confirmation, but he was sick. His legs were weak and he lay in bed or on the settee all day. He just about managed to get to the bathroom but couldn't walk more than a few steps without having to sit down. I loved having him at home where I could keep an eye on him.

After about ten days he was back to normal and he said it was a miracle. But something occurred to me today after reading an article in the *Guardian* by the neurologist Suzanne O'Sullivan. She has written a book, *The Sleeping Beauties*, about the phenomenon of psychosomatic illness. I am thinking now that it was a mental rather than a physical thing that was affecting him, and maybe the beginning of his troubles. It was a sign but one that I had no chance of recognizing.

Peter's employment was erratic. He was working as a labourer on a casual basis and was continually giving me the bad news that he had 'got his cards'. Usually he waited until dinner was over, which was good of him. I was always looking for work – typing, cleaning, being a home help – anything at all. As my own children grew, I began to look after other people's. Women out working or studying who needed a child minded were happy to employ me. Even with that, we never seemed to have enough money for everything. Some of Peter's family had ventured into the taxi business. Peter decided it might be the job for him and my brother agreed to be guarantor for a loan from the bank to buy the car, taxi meter and licence.

Peter becoming a taxi driver did not work out quite as I had hoped. Some days he would earn good money and bring it home. Other days he got distracted and spent time in the pub or the betting shop – or both. The loan at the bank wasn't getting paid and bills were piling up. We had the mortgage to pay, the electricity and the gas, and there never seemed to be enough to go round.

It wasn't all Peter's fault, I was just as bad. I found it almost impossible to deny him anything. A kiss and a cuddle and whatever I had in my purse was his.

What's that saying again? You know the one – when you keep making the same mistakes but keep persisting? It was Albert Einstein who said it: 'The definition of insanity is doing the same thing over and over again but expecting different results.' I don't think that occurred to Peter. He wasn't thinking about results, he merely pleased himself and hoped for the best. As for me, I just kept getting it wrong.

Still I love him, I'll forgive him, I'll go with him wherever he goes . . .

Just as long as he loved me. That was all that mattered.

outsider

People still ask me sometimes if I am on holiday. 'What do you think of Ireland?' they ask. It's my accent. I never lost it, that London twang. My brother-in-law Christie laughs at me when I say the word 'book'. 'It's a *boook*,' he says. I took one of my children to the doctor's surgery once. 'He's had a fall,' I said. 'A foal?' the doctor replied. 'Only horses produce foals.' It dogs me to this day. Taxi drivers are always asking me where I come from. 'Phibs-boro,' I reply, and they laugh.

I was on the 46a when a lady asked where had I come from. I told her, 'I got on in Dún Laoghaire,' and she laughed too. I told her then that I was born in London. 'You never lost your accent. Neither did I,' she said. I was puzzled because she sounded just like every other Dublin person to me. So I asked her where she was from.

'North Strand,' she said, 'can't you tell?'

I no longer have difficulty understanding the Irish accent after all these years, although if I go to the West of Ireland I have to listen intently. When I first came to Ireland, I missed BBC Radio 4. It is only since the internet that I can access it properly. Before that, I had a transistor radio that I used in bed. I kept it under the bedclothes because, for reasons I do not understand, I got better reception that way. If I became very lonely I listened to the cricket commentators; there is nothing more British than that.

I came to live in Ireland in 1962. At that time, the usual thing was for the Irish to emigrate to Britain or further afield. It was rare for the reverse to happen. I was twenty-three years of age, a Protestant, an outsider. It was an advantage in some ways because the people around me could not pin me down. They didn't know my background so I was an unknown quantity. But that went both ways: I didn't understand the religion, the politics or the ways of the Irish family, the Ingles, I had married into.

On my first Christmas Day in Dublin, I was expected to go to Mass. Everyone in the house was going and, although Mrs Ingle was aware that I was a Protestant, that didn't stop her from pushing me out of the door. Poor Tony, Peter's youngest brother, was given the job of escorting the English Protestant to Mass.

The last time I had been in church was when I got married. This time I didn't even manage to get inside because when we got to St Mary's Church in Haddington Road, it was full to overflowing. I turned to go, assuming that because there was no room in the church we would go elsewhere, just as Mary and Joseph had been obliged to do in Nazareth. But Tony held me back and so we stood outside the church in the freezing cold, along with the other latecomers, with the sound of strange mumblings coming from inside.

Tony instructed me to put on my mantilla. I had no idea what he was talking about. I looked around and saw the other women with black lace affairs on their heads. Tony produced a large white handkerchief from his pocket and draped it over my hair. In disbelief, I stood in the icy cold, outside the church, with a handkerchief on my head, watching people genuflecting and chanting in Latin.

I walked back to the house thinking how strange Irish people were. It was just the beginning of a long journey of discovery about the people who lived so close to England but were miles apart. We spoke the same language – well, nearly – but that was it.

Coming back to the house for the Christmas dinner nearly made up for the humiliating and baffling religious ceremony. Charlie, my father-in-law, sat at one end of the table carving, and generous amounts of turkey, ham and spiced beef were dispatched in the direction of our plates. Since he threw the meat, everyone had to extend their plates to catch it. No wine accompanied that dinner and, as I said, not a drop of brandy to anoint the Christmas pudding and set it alight. In my parents' house in London we had a sideboard which was fully stocked at Christmas and kept that way for the rest of the year. I didn't know then that, when they are confirmed, Catholic children are encouraged to 'take the pledge', promising not to drink alcohol until they are at least eighteen. In previous generations many people never took up drinking and remained Pioneers[1] for life.

---

1. Taking the confirmation pledge brought automatic membership of the Pioneer Total Abstinence Association, an Irish

When they were living at home, like their parents, none of the Ingles drank. They were a famous boxing family and keeping fit was instilled into them.[2] Peter didn't start to drink until he was eighteen. He had taken the pledge and, although he was far from home and away from the constraints of his Catholic upbringing, that early promise held him back. His brother John took to drinking alcohol when he went to New Zealand and Eddie when he joined the British army, but the rest stayed sober. Abstaining from alcohol isn't a bad idea considering the damage it can cause. I can say that now, as a wise old lady – too much gin in my tonic and I might

organization that encouraged members – Pioneers – to pray to the Sacred Heart of Jesus to help them stay away from alcohol. The PTAA still exists, but as the influence of the Church has declined, so has its membership.

2. When I phoned home from the telephone box, reversing the charges, the operator would invariably ask if I was 'anything to Jimmy Ingle?' In 1939, Peter's eldest brother, Jimmy, at the age of seventeen, was the first Irishman to win a European Amateur Boxing title. And Brendan, their younger brother, became a manager and boxing promoter as well as helping young people in Sheffield to change their lives for the better. When he died in May 2018 his funeral was attended by a representative of the President of Ireland and an emissary of Queen Elizabeth. A street in Sheffield is named after him – Brendan Ingle Way commemorates an extraordinary man who was much respected and loved by his community.

90

very easily tumble. But back then all I wanted was a flaming Christmas pudding.

I tried desperately to fit in. Everyone was very kind to me but still I felt like a stranger. And living with my in-laws brought with it an introduction to many things that would place me outside my comfort zone.

I will begin with the pigeons.

Charlie was a pigeon fancier and his birds were his pride and joy. I remember going up to the bedroom that first day and seeing them. I am not an animal lover, never visit zoos if I can help it, and birds, en masse, freak me out ever since I saw that Alfred Hitchcock film. Now here they were, lots of them, cooing in their house right outside the bedroom window and looking at me.

They slept at night but the noise of them during the day drove me demented and I couldn't understand how everyone else in the house could bear it. They kept telling me I'd get used to it but I didn't, not the noise, nor the smell of them.

Saturday was the day when the races took place and the big pigeon racing clock came out. I have to admit, they are very clever creatures – I would never be able to find my way home from France without directions, that's for sure.

Then there was the house cleaning. I was brought up in a very ordinary three-bedroom terraced house in London and there were never more than four of us in residence (and definitely no pigeons). Peter's house had been home to sixteen people at one stage. The place was spotless and, to maintain this standard, the cleaning process that took place on Friday evenings was mammoth and mainly undertaken by Bridget, Peter's sister. I didn't know if it was the Irish or just the Ingles who approached cleaning in a way that I had never before encountered. Every Friday the house would be turned upside down. I was obliged to take part in this weekly frenzy where everything had to be cleaned, whether it needed to be or not. Bridget was in charge and I, as her helper, would do as I was told.

I didn't mind polishing the trophies so much as I could sit at the table to do that and I didn't get in the way. There were an awful lot of them. The Ingles had excelled in everything from pigeon racing to hurling (an Irish sport I had never heard of; they told me it was a bit like hockey) to boxing and even ballroom dancing, and it was essential that those trophies were polished every week before being returned to the parlour. And when those wretched pigeons managed to arrive home before all the other birds, from Belgium or wherever they flew from, yet another trophy would appear.

The day they told me that the path at the front of the house had to be washed with a deck brush and a bucket of soapy water, I rebelled. I protested and said the rain would wash the path, and goodness knows there was enough of that. We argued and I gave in, all the time wondering as I scrubbed what my family back home would think of this madness.

And then there was shopping or 'going for the messages' as they called it.

The first time I went to buy chops I asked where the lamb came from. 'Is it New Zealand lamb?' I asked.

The man behind the counter looked at me as if I were simple. It wasn't my fault. Most of the lamb consumed in the UK was imported from New Zealand and my mother always told me it was the best.

'It comes from sheep,' the butcher said very slowly, 'sheep that are reared in Wicklow.'

One day, soon after, I actually saw sheep being herded for slaughter into the yard at the back of the shop. I felt such a fool.

Many of my favourite things were not available in Dublin. I missed croissants, olive oil, unsalted butter from Denmark, salt beef sandwiches, my mother's steak and kidney pie and Lyons tea shops.

Mrs Ingle was a good, plain cook and wholesome, fresh food was provided every day. Meat was served on most days, steak or pork chops, accompanied by cabbage or marrowfat peas, which had been soaked overnight, and of course potatoes. On Friday there was fresh fish. I learned a lot about fish from Mrs Ingle. The skinning of the ray, which I called skate, was a hard lesson. Placing the ray on newspaper so it wouldn't slip, she would make a small insertion under the skin and then, with her thumb, she prised it loose. Once a reasonable amount was free, she would take the newspaper in her hand and pull at the skin. On good days the whole skin would come off in one piece for her, but not for me. Still, I persevered, and lots of sore thumbs later I finally got it for life. It may not seem much of an accomplishment but try it and see how you get on.

Prawns like I had never seen before were often on the table on Friday evenings. Peter drove out to Howth and came back with sackfuls, which he bought for practically nothing. Mrs Ingle would have the big pot ready with boiling water and the prawns would be thrown in without ceremony and with only a little salt to accompany them. Minutes later, a pile of steaming prawns would appear on the table and then it was a free-for-all. They were fat and juicy and needed no other accompaniment – well, if they did, they never got it on those Friday evenings in Margaret Place.

Peter loved fish and seafood. When we had our own place he would go out to Bulloch Harbour and come home with crabs, live ones. I would spend hours picking out the flesh after boiling the poor things. Back in England, I had performed a similar job. My father used to have a drink in the Hare and Hounds every Sunday morning. Outside the pub there was a man who sold mussels, whelks, cockles and periwinkles. My father would bring home a pint of winkles and after dinner my job was to dewinkle them for tea. My spellchecker won't accept that as a word but how else to describe succinctly the task of inserting a needle into the winkle, carefully removing the flesh and discarding its little black hat? I then placed the winkles into small glasses full of vinegar to be eaten later with some lettuce and white bread and butter.

Pulling mackerel out of the sea in Mevagissey during my childhood was a regular event and I got used to handling their silky bodies, all blue, grey and white. At home in my great-aunt Em's house the heads would be removed and, without any ceremony apart from drying them with a clean cloth, they were thrown into the pan that was perched on the Primus stove. The big bone in the middle would come away easily when they were ready to eat. The smell of fresh fish frying, the sound of the crackle in the pan and Aunt Em tutting that she would never get the smell out of the kitchen were all part of the experience.

I was still living with my in-laws when Sarah was born in July 1963. Having an Irish child made me feel more settled, but I don't believe I have ever reached the heights of becoming the quintessential Irish Mammy.

Two days after Sarah arrived, Bridget, who was to be her godmother, arrived at my bedside in Holles Street and took Sarah to the chapel in the hospital to be baptized. The nurse reassured me that it was a Catholic tradition, since babies who died before being baptized did not go to heaven but to an in-between state known as limbo. I was afraid that they thought the child was about to die, but she told me not to worry.

'It's just a precaution,' she said.

That's all changed now, of course. It amazes me that the Catholic hierarchy can change the rules about eating fish on Friday and babies no longer going into limbo, but they can't change their minds about contraception being 'intrinsically evil' or the ordination of women.

After Sarah was born, I felt I had a purpose and pushed my new pram proudly. I'd take myself off for a walk, into town or down to Sandymount Strand, and the eyes of my mother-in-law would follow me.

'Where are you going?' she'd ask.

'Just out for a walk, get a bit of air,' I'd reply.

Of course, there were no mobile phones then, and they didn't even have a landline in the house, but before I returned my mother-in-law would know where I had been. Someone would have seen me along the way and reported back. Brinsley MacNamara's fictional *Valley of the Squinting Windows* had nothing on Bath Avenue.

Everything in Ireland was new to me and with no friends and very little in common with Peter's family, I felt out of place. I think they regarded me as a bit of an oddity and I certainly felt like one. When Peter took me to local swimming spots like the Shelly Banks or when we walked the South Wall to the Half Moon, I was happiest. Away from the house, alone with him, with the sea all around us was wonderful.

I swam at the Half Moon, which was meant for men

only, just to make a point. Usually the regulars weren't around at the time so my challenge to the patriarchy wasn't really that brave. If I got very homesick, Peter would take me out to Dún Laoghaire and buy me an ice cream from Teddy's and we would walk the East Pier.

'Where would you get it?' he would say to me as we looked out to sea. But my eyes kept wandering to that ferry that was setting off for Liverpool.

Once we bought our own house and the children came along, I began to feel more at home, although what other people thought of me, I don't know. That oft-repeated tale of what the British had done to the Irish for all those centuries haunted me. Now I could see it for myself and I was ashamed. In Derry on 30 January 1972, civil rights protesters were shot by members of the 1st Battalion of the British Parachute Regiment during a march in the Catholic Bogside. On that day, and many others during that time, I felt ashamed of my British heritage. Maybe it was my imagination, but I remember going into Brackens, a local supermarket, and a silence descending.

Religion was at the root of the troubles in the North but in Dublin it didn't seem to matter much that I was a Protestant. I lived beside Christ Church, the Methodist church, but I never thought of joining that congregation even though we always went to their sales of work and loved the biscuits. Those Protestant biscuits were the best, but I hated the Irel coffee – which tasted nothing like coffee – that they sold along with them.

When Sarah went to school in 1967 I asked the head-mistress, Sister Dolores, what they would be teaching her about religion. Sister Dolores replied in a very stern way, so typical of her, that if I was really that concerned, I should take instruction in the Catholic faith.

That was how I met Sister Agnes, who was to be my guardian angel and saviour for so many years. At our first meeting, I realized that Sister Agnes was not just educating me in the faith but was hoping for a conversion. Each Tuesday evening I walked to the convent and felt like a hypocrite. I had no intention of becoming a Catholic. I didn't even believe in God. But as the weeks went by, she wore me down. I became very attached to Sister Agnes and her sweet voice as she prayed over me and recited the 'Hail Mary' at the beginning and end of our meetings. If being a Catholic meant I could reach the dizzying heights of her goodness and simplicity of faith, surely it couldn't be a bad thing? She was always happy and smiling.

I found it difficult to accept the sacred mysteries of Catholic doctrine: the Holy Trinity, the Virgin birth, Christ's resurrection, transubstantiation. I argued with her and said they didn't make sense.

Sister Agnes had answers for everything and mostly they began and ended with faith. She urged me to attend Mass and to pray for the gift of faith. I hadn't prayed since I was a child when I had recited rapidly the prayer they taught me at Sunday School: *Now I lay me down to sleep, I pray the Lord my soul to keep; If I should die before I wake, I pray the Lord my soul to take. Amen.*

I went to Mass and started to pray, not just reciting 'Our Father' and the 'Hail Mary' but really trying to communicate with God on a personal level. I had been going through this ritual of weekly meetings, going to Mass and praying for six months or so when, as I walked down Durham Road to the convent, I felt moved by something outside of myself. When I saw Agnes that evening I told her I wanted to become a Catholic.

Looking back on this, I can see that the fear of dying was part of my wanting to believe. I didn't want to go into oblivion, I wanted to believe there was a heaven and that, if I did all the right things, I might qualify for admission. Three months later, I was received into the Catholic faith at the chapel in Lakelands Convent.

I had found the Catholic faith, but Sister Agnes had not initiated me into the pick-and-mix feature of the religion, whereby you didn't obey all the laws but made choices. The rule was that if you were a Catholic you should never use contraception as a means to regu-late your family. Many couples ignored this but, as a newcomer to the faith, I was not about to break a funda-mental directive. So, on 19 March 1969, our fifth child, Peter, was born.

I had come to Ireland an atheist, a socialist, a CND marcher, and now, six years later, I was a Catholic. I just gave in, if truth be told. It was more practical for me to be a Catholic in Ireland in those days. The schools were almost exclusively in the hands of nuns and priests. Being a Catholic meant I was part of a larger community and it allowed me to become a member of the board of management at the children's school and participate fully in their lives. 'Pragmatic' is the word that springs to mind.

In the mid 1980s, I was at Mass with some of the children and the priest urged the congregation to vote against a forthcoming amendment to the Constitution. The amendment proposed the deletion of Article 41.3 of the Constitution which stated that no law shall be enacted providing for the dissolution of marriage. Sarah was outraged that the priest had been so adamant in his demand that the congregation should vote against it. As we walked along Sandymount Road discussing it, she said she had to go and talk to the priest. She went back to the church and the priest reiterated all that he had said from the pulpit.

Sarah then sent a letter to the Pope and was answered by his ambassador in Ireland, the Papal Nuncio, to the effect that her thoughts had been noted. Sarah got married in a registry office in 1990.

I stayed a Catholic for some years, partly due to Sister Agnes and her big black bag, from which she produced much-needed funds for our family along with the *Sacred Heart Messenger*. Eventually, faced with the atrocities of the clergy, the terrible hidden treatment of unmarried mothers and the general hypocrisy around the wealth of the Church, I gave up.

I went to see Sister Agnes in June 2008, during the last weeks of her life, and most of my children, now adults, came with me. At the end it didn't matter what faith any of us held, we all loved her and said our tearful goodbyes. Agnes had been by my side through so much of my life with Peter and it was an honour to call her my friend.

When I was a Catholic I belonged to something. I think people need a sense of belonging and even today I envy people their faith. But recently I saw someone on Twitter writing about her mother needing more Masses said for her dead father so that he could get up to another level in purgatory. And that makes me sad.

I don't have one bit of faith or religion now. I think you have to make the most of this life. It is all we have. Kindness, generosity of spirit, tolerance and compassion for others are the tenets I strive to adhere to. I do not have to conform to any man-made rituals in order to be a Christian.

After living in Ireland for sixty years, I feel I belong here, it is my natural home. There are only two things I have yet to accept fully. One of them is timekeeping. Some Irish people have a terrible habit of arriving late. Their excuses very often make delightful stories but nevertheless they are not where they are supposed to be at the stipulated time.

When I met him first, Peter had a quaint saying: 'Now, in a minute.'

'How can it be "now" and "in a minute" all at the same time?' I would ask.

I found out when I moved to Ireland.

The other thing is directions. Sometimes people are over-optimistic as to how long it takes to get somewhere. 'It's just down the road,' or 'It'll only take you five minutes,' and you find yourself half an hour later wondering if they mistook you for Sonia O'Sullivan.

Apart from those two foibles, I am Irish. All the English has well and truly been extinguished. When the rugby Six Nations is on people ask me who I am looking to win, Ireland or England?

'Ireland, who else?' I reply. 'I'm Irish.'

Officially, I became an Irish citizen on 29 March 1977. I treasure that tiny document I received from the Department of Justice. I carry an Irish passport. I do not have dual citizenship, I am a citizen of Europe. And now, after this pandemic, when we are all in the same boat, I feel a part of the big wide world.

in pieces

My mother and father brought me on long holidays to Cornwall and sometimes left me there with my great-aunt Em. It rained a lot. There wasn't much to do. I was an only child on these holidays, while my older siblings were off living their own exciting lives.

To entertain myself, I read everything I could get my hands on. I discovered Jane Austen in Cornwall. Fell in love with the classics. We weren't a bookish family, but I became a reader over those long, lonely holidays.

And I loved jigsaws. I spent many solitary hours in Aunt Em's cottage in Mevagissey putting them together. They were magical, it seemed to me. You started off with a jumble of pieces and by the time you had finished, with patience and diligence, those pieces had become what ten-year-old me perceived as a work of art.

I know jigsaws aren't for everyone. But as a jigsaw lover I understand why they became so popular during the pandemic. In a time when we couldn't travel, with their lush landscapes and foreign landmarks, they offered an escape. Doing a jigsaw is a bit like meditating. There is no room for other thoughts when you are concentrating on conquering the challenge of vast expanses of blue sky or puffy white clouds. A jigsaw during a global crisis, when everything is so uncertain, is something that's within your control. It acts as a kind of therapy. I wish my eyes had been better during lockdown, I would have been a demon for the jigsaws. Instead, I knit ridiculous lockdown scarves.

Jigsaws were therapy for me when Peter's behaviour

became unbearable. He somehow got it into his head that I was flirting and having flings with other men. It happened over the course of several months. It crept up gradually until it came to a point where he constantly taunted and accused me, day after day.

When I painted the front door red, he said I was turning the place into a brothel. I thought he was joking at first. He accused me of seducing one of his best friends, of being too friendly with the coalman, the butcher, the milkman and even a kind garda who had helped to get him out of jail.[1]

This was 1972 and by now we had six children. How a woman with six children would have the time or the energy for such things did not seem to occur to him. I didn't understand. I was no Mata Hari. But I was a vulnerable and not unattractive young woman being treated badly by her husband; perhaps he thought other men might see that and chance their arm. His behaviour was cruel, unfair and bizarre. I couldn't understand what had come over him.

I could endure anything if I knew Peter loved me. But here was a man I did not recognize. He had suddenly and strangely changed his attitude. In the past, when he messed up, he had always been able to talk me round. Now, he didn't seem to care. I couldn't understand what I had done to deserve his contempt.

---

1. I tell this story in the chapter 'openhearted' on pp. 233–5.

I know now that this behaviour was an early mani-
festation of Peter's mental illness. But I didn't know that
at the time. He was imagining things that weren't really
happening. His poor head was bringing him to places I
couldn't visit or understand. All I saw was my husband
behaving as if he no longer wanted me around.

I had been through a lot with Peter but not being
loved or wanted by him was more than I could bear. The
children were suffering too. So, with no great drama, I
decided that if he didn't love me any more, I would set
him free.

I moved quickly. I wrote to my parents in Cornwall,
asking if I could come and live with them for a while. I
planned to leave at Easter, when the children got their
school holidays. I thought a few weeks away might
solve everything. Peter would surely come to his senses
and ask me to return home. In the meantime, I tried
to endure his hostility and attempted to save whatever
money I could for the big move.

I had taken to doing jigsaws in the evenings when the
children were in bed. We had no television and it tem-
porarily diverted me from the awfulness of everything.
One night, I went to bed leaving a 1,000-piece jigsaw
puzzle of the Houses of Parliament almost complete,
deliberately saving a few pieces for the next day. As jigsaw people know, there is nothing more satisfying than
slotting in those last few pieces of an especially difficult
puzzle.

When I came downstairs the next morning, I saw that Peter had put his hand into the middle of the jigsaw and scrunched it up, making a leaning tower of pieces in the centre. I saw it and I thought: *He must hate me.* He ruined my jigsaw. And even if it was the bastion of British politics staring up at him, he shouldn't have done it. It's funny how little things can tip you over the edge; this was my tipping point. Well, that and the punch.

It was a Sunday afternoon. Peter was sitting in the armchair, reading the paper. 'You have to go to work,' I said, 'we have no bread for the children's lunches.'

He ignored me, didn't even raise his head. I was so angry, I began to shout. I screamed at him but still he didn't answer. He just sat there as I kept up my tirade. Eventually he got up from the chair, put on his coat and made for the door. I followed him into the hall and, as he was leaving, he turned around and hit me full in the face, knocking me to the floor.

Peter had hit me for the first time. Like many women who are victims of domestic abuse, I am now about to make excuses for him: I shouldn't have spoken to him like that, but I was so full of rage at being ignored, I was out of control.

On the rare occasion I have a tendency to lose it completely and this was one of those times. Only a few months before, it would have been possible for me to sweet talk him into going to work, to cajole, kiss and flirt to get around him. Because he no longer loved me,

I couldn't do that. My womanly tricks wouldn't work any more.

Now I couldn't wait until Easter to get out of the house, to get away from him. I didn't yet have enough money saved for the fare. Brazenly, I asked Tony Dowling, the local butcher, if he could lend me some cash. I didn't exactly spell out what I was intending to do, but I think he got the message. My black eye might have given him a clue. I told my good friend Sister Agnes of my plans and, although she wasn't happy, she didn't try to dissuade me.

I had made up my mind that we were never coming back and I just wanted a clean break. I gave the children's toys away to my neighbour and she asked no questions. What lay ahead of me was the monumental task of transporting myself and six children to Cornwall. It's hard to imagine this now because these days going into town on my own on the no. 9 bus, clutching my bag for life, is a major expedition.

I packed two suitcases with as many of our clothes as I could manage to fit. I didn't have a sling for the baby, as many young women have today, so I had to carry Róisín and my hands would be full. 'You have your hands full there,' was a constant comment from observers, even when I wasn't running away from home. I was up very early to make sandwiches for the journey and bottles for the baby. As we washed and dressed, I urged the children to be quiet, so as not to wake Peter. Sarah was eight, the twins six, Rachael five, Peter three and baby

Róisín just five months old. I was thirty-three years of age and about to become a single mother.

I left a note on the table telling Peter that I was leaving, alongside an article from the *Irish Press* written by Mary Kenny about alcoholics and the suffering of their families. Mary Kenny has changed her stance on so many things that she is not someone I would now look to for advice and guidance, but at the time she was one of my heroines. I don't know if Peter bothered to read it or if it was even relevant to a man who had, apparently, fallen out of love with his wife.

I thought at the time that the drink was Peter's problem. I was ignorant and knew little about alcoholism. Peter never drank at home and it was usually only pints of Guinness he had in the pub. But he was fond of the saying 'A bird never flew on one wing' and stuck by it: for him, it was no use going into a pub and only having the one pint. The drink never really agreed with him and, more often than not after a night out, he would either get up with a hangover or stay in bed and nurse it.

We crept out of the house that cold spring morning and huddled together in the taxi bound for the docks. The children were all very good, excited at the unexpected activity, and why wouldn't they be? Instead of going to school they were getting on a boat to England and who knew what adventures lay ahead. They didn't ask any questions. The last few months had been as hard for them as for me.

The journey to Liverpool took seven hours. By the time we got there, it was beginning to get dark, and I had no idea of where we would sleep. My careful planning hadn't gone that far. I hailed a taxi and asked the driver if he knew of a cheap place we could stay for the night. He took us to a lodging house that was situated in a rundown part of the city. As I lay awake listening to the doors in that house opening and closing, I realized I had landed us in what is colloquially known as a 'knocking shop'.

The next day, we were up early to catch the first of many trains. From Liverpool, we changed at Crewe, Birmingham and Exeter before we reached St Austell. It was an eventful journey with lots of games of I Spy, little hands waving out of the window to anyone and everyone, bottles of lemonade and cheese and pickle sandwiches consumed, with naps in between. As I watched over my children and the wheels of the train ran along the tracks, they seemed to be saying, over and over: *Have you done the right thing? Have you done the right thing? Will it all be okay? Will it all be okay?*

At St Austell, we got a bus to Mevagissey. We must have looked a sight as we struggled along from the bus stop to my parents' house, bedraggled and travel-worn. They had arranged beds for us in the large attic of the house and we all slept soundly that night, waking the next morning to the cries of seagulls.

Soon after we arrived, I enrolled the older children in

the local school while Peter and Róisín stayed at home with me. The children were my first concern and the move hadn't proved too traumatic for them as far as I could see. I applied for social welfare and put my name down for a council house in the area.

I knew from the beginning it wasn't going to be easy for me to make a new life for myself in Cornwall, but, in spite of everything, I believed I had made the right decision. If Peter didn't want me then what was the point of being with him? But I missed Ireland and him.

When it finally sank in that we were really gone, Peter started telephoning, and he called most every night. At first he was angry, saying that I had taken his children away and I couldn't do that. He threatened legal action, but I knew Peter couldn't pay the electricity bill, never mind hire a solicitor.

And then he started pleading with me to come home.

8 Sandymount Green
Dublin 4
22 April 1972

Dear Ann

Just getting myself right again after yesterday. I got very drunk. On the phone last night you said that you wanted to forget me. Were you really serious Ann or were you just trying to annoy me. I have been working all afternoon and I am looking forward to ringing you tonight. What do you think, Ann, what do you

*really want to do. Do you love me Ann . . . all that I know
is that I want to be with you and that is love as far as I am
concerned, no matter what you think or no matter what you want
to do. If you think you are right when you are doing something,
you might be wrong. I understand and that is what matters
because women have a different way of thinking than men.*

    *I did not treat you right and I am paying for it and that
is that. You are a beautiful, full blooded woman. I can't stop
thinking about you Ann, all the time you are on my mind. I
can't even sleep without thinking about you and if that is not
loving someone well I don't know anything about love. Do you
think about me as much?*

    *I said to you last night that I would send you the fare to come
back . . . we could work things out better if we were together
although it might take a bit longer. What do you think Ann?*

Well, what did Ann think? I was in a terrible muddle.
Try as I might, I couldn't stop loving him. But loving
someone doesn't mean you have to leave yourself open
to abuse. Peter's letters and telephone calls were frustrating because sometimes he was reasonable and loving,
other times he was like a spoilt child who couldn't have
what he wanted.

When the telephone calls and letters didn't get him
anywhere, Peter decided to come in person. The day
he arrived at the house, I thought my father would be
furious and turn him away. He didn't let him in but
instead the two of them went to The Fountain, my dad's

favourite pub. My mother and I sat waiting, wondering what was happening.

Whatever went on between them, I'll never know, but they came back the best of friends, with a mutual respect having been established. My mother and I were in a state of shock and couldn't believe our ears as they laughed and joked together. 'Typical men,' you might say, but these two were not typical of any men I have ever known, before or since.

I tried to remain calm and indifferent to his presence, but when I saw how delighted the children were to see their father, it was difficult. They hung on to him and dragged him down to the little beach in the harbour to catch crabs. In the evening, Peter and I went out together and walked up the hill overlooking the harbour. That same harbour I see in the painting on the wall today.

Peter wanted me to pack up there and then and go back with him to Ireland. He stayed for three days and by the end of that time he had won me over with his promises and kisses. We came to an agreement: if Peter would send me the fare for us all to return to Ireland, then I would come home.

The money was cobbled together, some sent by Peter and the rest from my father. I was apprehensive but excited at the same time. I had missed Ireland. In England, when you go out for a drink and people ask will you have another, and you – out of politeness and not wanting to appear greedy – say no, you stay thirsty. In

Ireland, like Mrs Doyle in *Father Ted*, it would be 'Go on, go on, ah you will,' and the drink would appear before you like magic. I missed the openness and generosity of spirit, the spontaneous wit, the slagging and, most of all, Peter.

Peter met us at the airport and brought us home in the taxi. When we entered the house, I couldn't believe my eyes. Nothing had changed, except that now a layer of dust and dirt had accumulated and everything I touched felt cold, damp and dirty. Peter had made no effort to make it welcoming for us and tears came to my eyes as I looked at the unwashed dishes in the sink. The note I had left on the kitchen table was still lying there, and Mary Kenny's face was looking up at me.

I swept the floor, got a bucket of hot water from the geyser in the bathroom and started trying to make the place habitable. As I mopped, I began to regret my decision to return. The bathroom Peter had started to build upstairs was still a gaping hole and far from completion. Downstairs, that bathroom in the old outhouse was the bane of my life – we might as well have been washing ourselves in the garden for all the protection those skimpy walls gave us.

One Saturday, about two weeks after we came home, the gas boiler over the bath failed to ignite. My neighbour, May Smyth, kindly said I could bathe the children at her house. This was a great treat because the Smyths had a television and as each child got bathed and dressed in their nightclothes they went downstairs into the sitting room to watch *Skippy the Bush Kangaroo*.

While I was bathing the children at May's, Peter came home to find an empty house. He had been gone since early that day. I had been expecting him home with the meat he had promised to buy from a butcher in Thomas Street. When he came into the house to find none of us there, he immediately thought I had left him again. Peter knew there was no boat at that time of the day so he drove out to the airport. When he couldn't find us there, he was frantic and called into his mother's in case we had gone to visit her.

Finally, he came home to find all the children in bed and me still there waiting anxiously for him. Mad passionate kisses ensued, a roast for tomorrow's dinner was produced and we went happily to our bed. The empty house had given him a shock and things improved.

Later that year, a local benefactor, Cartan Finegan, offered me a week's holiday in a beautifully painted wooden caravan he had bought from a Traveller. It was parked right on the beach in Rush, County Dublin. I didn't realize it at the time, but everyone in the neighbourhood must have known we were struggling, hence his generosity. We piled into the car and spent seven blissful days there. Peter was back in love with me again and another child was conceived in that caravan. Michael was born in April 1974 and we were delighted with our new son. When he was baptized, though Mr Finegan was not present, he was named as Michael's godfather. I didn't tell Mr Finegan that until many years later. When you have a big family, it is easy to run out of nominees for the position of godparent.

Peter drove us all to Rush for that holiday but went back to Dublin to 'work' most days. From the beginning of his career as a taxi driver, in between picking up paying passengers, he had used the car to facilitate his social life. He loved meeting and talking to people. He became friendly with Luke Kelly of The Dubliners, who he met in O'Donoghue's in Merrion Row. He brought him home one day to show off the children – and me too, I suppose. We all went for a drive and a walk to the Poolbeg Lighthouse, the two of them singing to the sea at the top of their voices.

Peter sang anywhere and everywhere. He entered singing competitions and made the final at the International Hotel in Bray. He wanted to perform Engelbert Humperdinck's 'Please Release Me (Let Me Go)', which he sang as well as Engelbert. For obvious reasons, I hated the lyrics. I persuaded him to sing a Frankie Vaughan number. I can see him now as he rehearsed 'You're Nobody Till Somebody Loves You' with a bauble from the Christmas tree in his hand as a pretend mike and the children sitting on the floor in front of him as his audience. Peter came second to a soprano with a very high-pitched voice.

It was through Luke Kelly that Peter met John Molloy, one of The Dubliners' first promoters. He was a great raconteur, actor and writer, and a seventh-generation Dubliner, or so he told me. One Saturday afternoon, Peter brought him home after pints in the pub on Sandymount Green. They were hungry and could smell the corned beef I was cooking for the next day's dinner. I made sandwiches for them with the hot beef, mustard and a batch loaf. They called for more until it was all gone. I could do no wrong in John Molloy's eyes ever after.

Sometimes, there were family outings in the taxi. Peter drove us to the Powerscourt Estate to see the gardens and the waterfall. When we came to the entrance, where we were expected to stop and pay the admission fee, he kept going and drove through at top speed, much to the delight of the children.

'We have to pay,' I said.

'We do not,' he replied. 'The land belongs to the people of Ireland.'

In fact, the land belonged to the Slazenger family who had bought it from the 9th Viscount of Powerscourt in 1961.

We were on safer ground when we drove out to Brittas Bay as the beach really did belong to everyone. We swam and made sandcastles, and Peter told the children that this was the place where St Patrick landed when he first came to Ireland. And who was I to question that?

Unfortunately, Peter's working life continued to go

downhill. He would leave the taxi in inappropriate places while he went to the betting shop or the pub. Very often he went to Shelbourne Park, the greyhound stadium, before proceeding to the Lansdowne Bar or Nolan's in Bath Avenue. Once he started to sing, a pint would be pulled and he never had to put his hand in his pocket to buy the next one.

All our outings and Peter's adventures came to an end when An Garda Síochána unceremoniously took back Peter's taxi licence. We got advice from a local solicitor and tried to get the decision reversed, but we were unsuccessful. Not long after, the car was repossessed, so it didn't matter anyway. No licence, no car, no job. Peter signed on at the unemployment office.

He was angry at first with losing the licence and the car but soon settled into this new way of life. I continued to do any work that came my way – typing, childminding, cleaning – but I became more prudent. I hid money from Peter, sometimes under the lino. He walked on top of it as he pleaded with me for the price of a pint. And, in between it all, he was lovely. I loved him, we all did. Everybody did.

Peter was an enigma. The biggest, hardest puzzle I ever came across. The pieces just wouldn't fit together no matter how hard I tried.

educating ann

In my childminding years, I looked after a little boy called David while his mother, Kate, went off to Trinity College to study English. As Kate left each day, I looked after her longingly and then went back into the house to make another batch of playdough. I envied her.

I was continually saying how much I would love to go back to college, and one day, exasperated, my son-in-law Willo, usually so polite, said, 'Why don't you do it, so, and stop talking about it?'

'It's not that easy,' I said. I knew if I really wanted it, I had to make it happen.

In 1990, at the age of fifty-one, I made plans to fulfil my lifelong ambition to obtain a degree. Some of my children had been successful – surely I could do it too?

I applied to University College Dublin and Trinity College Dublin.

As a prospective mature student, TCD requires you to sit an examination, which I duly did. I thought I did quite well but, apparently, I wasn't good enough. Not making excuses or anything, but Trinity only accepted ten mature students a year at that time. UCD didn't want me either.

Undaunted – well, not too daunted – I enrolled in a Pre-University Course at Pearse College in Crumlin, where I studied history, English and psychology. They call it a University Access Course now. It was a small class and some students dropped out after the first few weeks, but I loved it. What I learned in that year has stood to me for the rest of my life. I passed the end-of-term examinations and, armed with the certificate I had obtained, I once again applied to Trinity College and UCD. Maynooth University, I decided, was out for me as it was too far away. Trinity was just a short bus ride and my preferred option.

I turned up for the mature students' entrance exam once again. It was easier for me this time having had a year of academic study. I was confident that I would succeed.

I didn't. I was turned down again by both Trinity College and UCD.

I nearly gave up. I had spent a whole year studying and still the bastions of higher education denied me entry. I decided to enrol at Ringsend Technical College to study for the Leaving Certificate. They have a programme for students to repeat the Leaving and, although I had never sat it in the first place, they were willing to take me on. I wanted to do home economics because I knew that would be an easy one. However, you were not allowed to take home economics in just one year and so I settled for business studies, economics, mathematics, English and history.

Business studies was easy enough, economics was a nightmare, mathematics was a challenge, history was hard work and English was my favourite subject. I was the only mature student in the class. I sat beside young people of seventeen and eighteen years of age who, unlike me, were actually repeating their Leaving. They didn't seem to mind and neither did I, but I found being older than some of the teachers a little disconcerting.

I passed the Leaving Certificate with one A, three

Bs and a D (damn that economics). This time I applied through the Central Applications Office and Trinity finally accepted me. I think they must have realized I was never going to give up.

The degree I opted for was history and English. I studied history for the first two years but I soon realized that I had made a mistake. I'd had a brilliant teacher, Dan Bradshaw, in Pearse College. He made it all so interesting and I was convinced that the study of history would be exciting and worthwhile. It wasn't. Some of the lecturers had been churning out the same old stuff for years. Well, history is like that, I suppose. There were one or two younger lecturers who went in for 'deconstruction'. I was never really sure what to make of their reinterpretation of historical facts.

One lecturer was always late for lectures and looked as if he had just got out of bed. His study was the epitome of an absent-minded professor's. I went into his office one day to discuss an essay I was writing and had to move a pile of papers before I could sit down. He told me it was difficult to keep on top of things and asked would I like the job of tidying it up. I picked up my bag, made some excuse and left.

Before year three began, I took advantage of the J1 visa as a student and went to America for the first time in my life. I had one son in Seattle, one in San Francisco and one in Winston-Salem, North Carolina, at the time. Michael, who was in San Francisco, lived on a houseboat.

I wouldn't have minded, but it was moored way out to sea in order to avoid paying berthing fees. I definitely would not have been able to row to work each day, so that was out. Winston-Salem didn't sound too exciting, so I decided that Peter in Seattle was the best option.

Although I was a mature student and in my fifties, as far as the J1 visa authorities were concerned, I was a young person. This meant that I had to travel on the plane with all the other students, stay overnight with them in Columbia University in New York and be subjected to a lecture on how to behave properly in America before I could continue on to Seattle.

Getting a job was easy, I just took a test in an employment agency. I was typing a hundred words a minute at that time, so they thought I was quite brilliant.

I loved Seattle, a city surrounded by water on all sides. The sea, the river and the lakes were beautiful and the snow-capped Mount Rainier in the distance never ceased to enchant me as I walked to work. Peter took me to Vancouver for the day, which enables me to boast that I have been to Canada. I went for the weekend to see Michael in San Francisco and stayed with Eddie for a week in North Carolina on my way home.

When I resumed my studies, it was in the English Department. Hearing David Norris give his lectures on Joyce was a theatrical experience, but I never actually got around to reading *Ulysses*. Brendan Kennelly, with his

Kerry accent and stories which seemed to have nothing to do with the syllabus as far as I could make out, captivated the young women.

I recently came across a book published by Lilliput Press, *Trinity Tales: Trinity College Dublin in the Nineties*, in which '40 young shapers and makers of contemporary Ireland' write of their experiences. I was interested because I was there at the time. Professor Diarmaid Ferriter described the book as 'dripping with privileged nostalgia', but his alma mater was UCD so that might account for the scathing comment.

It was a revelation to me that writers and performers such as Claire Kilroy, Belinda McKeon, John Boyne, Turtle Bunbury, Trevor White, Dominic West and Mario Rosenstock were all floating around the place as I was struggling to keep up. They were in the embryonic phase of their starry careers. I wouldn't have bumped into them anyway because I did not frequent the Buttery or Pavilion bars. I hadn't a minute to spare.

At the same time as studying, I was running a mini word-processing bureau from my bedroom. There was no shortage of work and my Dictaphone enabled me to take dictation from solicitors, barristers, plastic surgeons and architects. Some of my clients were fellow students of my son Peter, who was studying at the College of Marketing. Dissertations were churned out as the students came to their final year. Whoever needed me, I was there. As a mature student I didn't have to pay fees at Trinity but I still had to keep the house going. I couldn't manage that on the weekly Widow's Pension of £85.

I often felt intimidated by some of my fellow students, especially in tutorials. There was a particular young lady (she could have been one of those I've mentioned for all I know) whose vocabulary was extensive. Her parents were teachers and, coincidentally, her uncle was the untidy history man I mentioned earlier. She used words that were foreign to me. Imagine having to surreptitiously make a note of a word spoken by an eighteen-year-old so that you could look it up later.

It wasn't just her, of course. There were so many literary terms that tripped off the tongues of the lecturers and the more studious students. I have to tell you that, to this day, whenever I hear the word 'postmodern', shivers run down my spine. I was cheered to hear Marian Keyes on Instagram the other day saying how little she knew of literary jargon, and she's a world-famous writer. Words that were used as common currency were alien to me, words like 'redaction', 'anapaest' (a metrical foot consisting of two short or unstressed syllables followed by one long or stressed syllable), 'bathos', 'dactyl' and 'irony'. I always thought I knew what that one was. Ironically, I was wrong.

I made friends with some of the young students; I was handy to know because I attended all the lectures and they often asked to borrow my notes.

My dissertation was on the emasculation of men during the First World War. It was a study of the 'Regeneration' trilogy written by Pat Barker. I enjoyed doing that, but the exams were a nightmare. I sat in that big examination hall to write answers to questions such as 'Discuss how the narrative voice affects the way we read the Victorian novel' or 'What significant psychoanalytic theories do you see in the work of Conrad?' For years after, I never took the shortcut through Trinity to get to Dawson Street – passing the Examination Hall in Front Square gave me the jitters.

I graduated from Trinity in 1997, aged fifty-eight, a degree under my oxter and a smile on my face. Despite all the odds, my perseverance had got me into college and hard work had seen me finish. But at the end of it all, when the excitement had died down and the gown was returned, I was disappointed. I had thought that spending four years in Trinity College would make me an intellectual, but I didn't feel any different. I had learned how to structure an essay so that I could receive good marks. I had learned how to read quickly, skim through things and make succinct notes. I had read a vast number of books and, occasionally, I am even able to answer the literary questions on *University Challenge*.

But I didn't feel any different. Four years in Trinity was no *Educating Rita* for me. No Michael Caine at the end of the rainbow. Don't get me wrong, I don't regret it. It was a wonderful experience and a privilege, but I was still the same person at the end of it all.

Financially, there were benefits. A company that I had previously worked for as a typist offered me a job as the production manager on a new educational project. I could have done that job without a degree, but the BA after my name gave me the status that would justify a few thousand pounds a year more than a typist.

Having a degree in English was one of the credentials I presented to Rosemary Smith when we met in the Fitzwilliam Hotel in 2016. She wanted someone to ghostwrite a book about her life and career as a rally driver. The writer Paul Howard had put me in touch with her. He thought that as we were of the same vintage – she was seventy-nine and I was seventy-seven – we would be a good fit. Our ages are similar, but we have very little else in common. Rosemary is tall and slim and very glamorous. As well as being a fantastic driver, she was a model in her day. I am short and generously proportioned, definitely not mannequin material. We took to one another nevertheless. Rosemary wasn't interested in my degree, it meant nothing to her. She just liked me.

I went home and googled 'how to be a ghostwriter', which was of little use. I do not drive a car and knew nothing about rallies or motor racing. I did a lot of reading and spent a year and a half meeting Rosemary once a week at 11 a.m. at the Royal Irish Automobile Club, recording every word she said. That way, I became familiar with her way of saying things. I had to tell her story in *her* voice and lose mine. *Driven* was published by Harper-Collins and launched by Paul in October 2018. Rosemary says she doesn't just like me now, she loves me.

normal people

My husband was always an unconventional man with little regard for authority. When he still had the car we were out for a drive one day when he drove up a one-way street in Bray and we were stopped by a garda.

'Did you not see the signs?' the garda asked as I rolled down the window.

'Signs of what?' Peter said innocently. 'Signs of what?'

And you might ask me the same question: *Did you not see the signs?*

I accepted Peter for who he was, someone a bit different from the rest. He wasn't your normal, average person. But, really, which one of us is? We all have our funny ways.

But then, one fateful day, Peter's behaviour was a little too much out of the ordinary.

The window of the front room of our house was big, out of proportion when viewed from the outside, but that was the way Peter had made it when we moved in. He wanted more light in the sitting room, he said, he wanted to see the trees in the Green, and it didn't bother him what it looked like from the outside. Though no. 8 Sandymount Green was over a hundred years old, it had few merits architecturally, inside or out, so it didn't matter to me either.

Peter and I were sitting in the front room on a dismal morning in December 1975. He hadn't been feeling well. Headachy, he said. There were no children to mind that day and I went out to the kitchen to make us tea. As

I walked back into the room, mugs in hand, I saw him staring out of the window and laughing.

'What are you looking at, Peter?' I asked.

'It's great that there are so many people out there in the Green in the sunshine. They look like they're having a good time.'

I looked over his shoulder. There was nobody in the Green. There was no sunshine on that dull, grey day.

I put down the mugs and held him in my arms.

We sat together on the settee drinking our tea. He was happy and smiling. His headache was gone. Mine was just beginning.

'I think we should go to see Dr Power,' I said.

'What for? I'm fine. Are you ill?' he said.

'I have a pain in my side,' I said, trying to convince him that going to the doctor was a good idea. 'He can look at us both. Peter, you're not yourself.'

He wasn't himself. Who was this man who was seeing things that weren't there and frightening the life out of me?

So, we went to see Dr Power and after a brief discussion he decided that Peter was suffering from delirium tremens.

That can't be right, I thought. Peter hadn't seen pink elephants – just people who weren't there and a sky full of sunshine and light. I wasn't convinced that he was an alcoholic.

Dr Power referred Peter to Dr Stevenson, the Clinical Director of St Dympna's at St Brendan's Psychiatric

Hospital, Grangegorman, formerly known as the Richmond Lunatic Asylum. St Dympna's was a clinic for drug addicts and alcoholics.

Peter went to the clinic. He took the prescribed tablets, Disulfiram (Antabuse). He was told that if he drank alcohol while he was taking them he would become violently sick. He didn't seem to mind.

'Not drinking doesn't bother me,' he said. This coming from a man who loved the pub and the craic surprised me.

One of his friends was very upset when Peter wasn't to be seen at the pub. He called to the house to take him out for a pint but Peter refused his offer.

'You wanna be careful,' the man said. 'You'll go mad if you give up the drink. It happened to my brother.'

Peter was sober and happy. I tried to persuade myself that the episode of the laughing, happy people he saw in the Green was just an aberration. Maybe the doctor was right. Maybe he'd had a touch of the dreaded DTs and that's all it was. But, still, I had my doubts.

Peter went to the meetings at the clinic every week, to the unemployment office and out for walks. But things were changing. When he was at home, he would sit for hours just staring into space.

'What's wrong, Peter?' I asked.

'Nothing wrong,' he said, 'I'm just thinking.'

Day after day, just thinking. It wasn't like Peter at all. I was grateful that he wasn't drinking, that his unemployment money came home intact and that I saw more of him than I had in years. I went about my business minding children, cooking, cleaning, all the usual mundane stuff, while Peter sat oblivious to it all. He never talked about his drinking pals or bothered to seek them out. He was like a lost soul, unsure of where he was or what he was doing.

Maybe he's just lonely, I thought. He'd had so many friends when he was drinking but now they were gone and all he had was me and the children.

I was worried about him and went to see our doctor again. He told me that everything would be all right. He said that Dr Stevenson was an expert and these things take time.

So I waited.

It was when Peter started to go to Mass every day that I knew something was seriously wrong. He didn't go to the local Star of the Sea Church but to Our Lady Queen of Peace on Merrion Road. I don't know how to explain it, but it was as if I were living with a different man.

Peter changed again. He became animated once more, but all he wanted to talk about was God, religion and the Catholic Church. All the time. He came home with pamphlets entitled 'Hell and Punishment', 'Divorce is a Disease', and he insisted I read them. He was like an evangelist, and when the children were in bed he wanted me to read every word out loud to him. Then he would go over it again, explaining it all to me as if I were unable to understand.

The pamphlet he kept returning to was the one about Matt Talbot, the Dublin man who was an alcoholic until, at the age of twenty-eight, he took a solemn pledge to stop drinking. I can remember all the details, I heard it so many times. When Matt Talbot died he was taken to hospital, where they discovered the chains and cords he had wound around his body. Peter read it over and over again. He was fascinated by him.

'He was a great man,' he told me. 'He slept on a plank at night as a penance.'

'That old mattress of ours is bad enough, don't even think about it,' I said. But Peter wasn't laughing.

He did everything in a hurry now. The lethargic Peter of a few weeks earlier had gone. I had no choice but to listen to him and try to keep calm.

'I am embracing my religion, you should be happy for me,' he said.

One Sunday he didn't come home until after we had all eaten. When he did arrive he told me he was late because he had been to three Masses in the church, one after the other.

'Sit down,' he said, 'I've something very important to tell you.'

'I've heard it all, Peter, I'm getting tired of all this religion.'

He insisted, so we sat at the kitchen table. He spoke calmly, slowly and distinctly.

'I am being eaten inside by the devil. He is eating away at me. I can feel it.'

I can remember the cold feeling that came over me. That total inability to think my way out of it made me shiver.

As he continued talking, I attempted to humour him. I would have said anything at that moment to make it all stop. So what did I say?

'You're just hungry, eat your dinner.'

Peter was telling me that the devil was eating his insides and that was all I could come up with.

Peter needed me to believe him. How do you tell someone that what they are feeling isn't real? You can't. I just said, 'I know it's real for you, but it's hard for me to take it in,' and hoped for the best.

He didn't eat his dinner.

On Monday he was going in to see Dr Stevenson. I told Peter to tell him all about his experience. 'He will know what to do,' I said, 'he'll help you.' That's what I hoped because I was at a loss to know what to say or do. It was all too much.

The next day I waited for Peter to come home. Maybe Dr Stevenson would have waved a magic wand, or at least given him a Valium or something.

Directly he walked in I could see that neither of those things had happened. Peter paced around the kitchen, getting in the way as I was cooking dinner. He wanted me to stop and listen to him.

'We have to eat,' I said, 'the children are hungry.'

I didn't want them to hear him talk about devils eating him or whatever else he might come out with.

'It's important,' he said. 'I have to tell you now, immediately.'

'Wait,' I said, 'be patient. We will have time to talk later.'

I tried to sound calm and normal, but I was shaking inside.

Peter sat at the table, but he hardly ate any food and his pleading eyes followed my every move.

I managed to get through that dinner, put the dishes in the sink and went upstairs with the children. I dallied over their stories and songs, dreading having to face Peter again. Looking back, I should have got help there and then, but I didn't know. How could I?

Peter was waiting for me in the sitting room with his head in his hands. He stood up when he saw me and gently took my hand and drew me on to the settee beside him. I was glad that he had calmed down. Maybe everything was all right. I cuddled up beside him, hoping for the best.

Peter began to talk in a soft voice, in a cajoling way as if he were speaking to a child.

'I need your help,' he said. 'You must listen carefully.'

'I'd do anything for you, Peter, you know that.'

'I have something to tell you,' he said. 'You must

believe me even though it might be hard for you. Don't be afraid.'

He held my hand and gazed at me with his clear blue eyes.

'I am Jesus Christ. My father, Charlie, is God and my niece Tracy is the Virgin Mary.'

He paused then, waiting for my reaction. He had said that sentence in such a matter-of-fact, sincere and convincing way, you might almost think it was true. I really wanted to say I believed him as it would make things so much easier. Just saying, *Yes, of course, Peter, I always knew that*, or some such mad thing.

I told him to wait. One of the children was calling, I said. But I ran upstairs to the toilet to relieve myself. It's true what they say about fear and bowel movements.

When I came back down, Peter kept talking, saying it over and over again. 'I am Jesus, you must believe me.' He was begging me, trying to make me understand.

'It's very hard for me, Peter, can't you see that?' I said, trying to play for time. What he said in reply were the most terrifying words I have ever heard or will ever hear.

'It will soon be Easter, you must understand what I have to do. I must die to save the world. You and the children will come with me.'

I listened in bewilderment and terror.

'We have to make this sacrifice,' he said, 'it's the only way.'

I listened, pretending that I understood and willing

him to keep on talking to give me time to think. I began to talk too, wildly, saying anything to make him stop, but it didn't work.

This went on for what seemed like forever until he said, quite calmly, 'Fetch me a knife.'

I felt like breaking into hysterical laughter. I wanted to remind him that the knives in our house couldn't cut butter, as he well knew.

I tried to pacify him. I said I would get the knife but it would take me a while to find the right one. I was desperate to stay by his side and keep him talking. I wanted to run to the neighbours' to telephone for help, but I couldn't take the risk.

If this was a story you wouldn't believe what happened next. There was a knock on the door and there was Mary, the mother of one of the children I minded. Mary was a psychiatric nurse.

'Peter,' I said, 'Mary has come. Tell her everything.'

Mary sat listening. This was not what she was expecting. She had only come to tell me what time she would deliver her daughter the next day.

Peter was eager to tell her everything. He repeated it all. He said that he was ready to make the supreme sacrifice, that he was Jesus and that Ann and the children must go to heaven with him.

Mary was familiar with people with delusions but it was generally within hospital walls, with other staff around her and tranquillizers at the ready. There was little

she could do here in my sitting room, but we were buying time.

I never usually had visitors in the evening but, by some
miracle, minutes later, a second friend arrived. It was
Audrey, another mother whose children I looked after.

Now there were three of us and Peter seemed to enjoy
having an audience. He relaxed and again, quite calmly,
he spelled out his horrific plans. As long as we sat there
listening to him, acting like three of the apostles, he was
happy. I tried to make a move for the door but each time
he told me to sit down.

Mary and Audrey attempted to persuade him that he
was unwell and needed help. Peter didn't like that. He
expected everyone to believe him and what they were
saying was not what he wanted to hear. His mood
changed and he became angry. He began shouting and
roaring at us to leave him alone. He was on his feet now
and suddenly he threw himself violently at the fireplace
like a raging bull towards a matador, head down. Peter
had made that fireplace himself with big grey stones he
had transported from Howth. It was a work of art, a
handmade fireplace that nobody else would ever have,
he used to say. And now here he was throwing himself at
it in his frustration and anger, cutting his beautiful head
with each lunge.

The three of us flung ourselves at him and grappled
him to the floor. We lifted the big coffee table, placed it
on top of him and sat on it. Peter was trapped and, as he

twisted and shouted to be released, I ran to my neighbour next door to telephone for an ambulance. I left Mary and Audrey sitting on the table, with Peter screaming like a wild animal underneath them.

I went with him to St Brendan's and Mary stayed behind to mind the children as Audrey followed in her car. At the hospital, nurses dressed his bleeding head and, as he started again to become agitated, they gave him an injection to calm him down.

We were brought into a room to see the psychiatrist, who questioned Peter. He asked him, 'What year is it?', 'Who is the President of Ireland?', and Peter answered correctly, without hesitation.

I felt like shouting at the doctor: *He knows all that, his problem is he thinks he's Jesus Christ, for God's sake! He thinks me and our children have to die for the world's sins.*

But, of course, I said none of that. When the doctor asked him if he would voluntarily sign himself into St Brendan's that night, and Peter lifted the pen to do so, it was a great relief.

I telephoned Dr Stevenson in St Dympna's the next morning. He told me that when Peter had attended the clinic the previous day, he had created a disturbance by standing up at the meeting and delivering a sermon. Apparently, he had told everyone that they had to repent and, if they did, he would save them. Then he had left and come home to me and my seven children.

Peter was obviously delusional and, as it turned out,

he was a danger to himself and everyone around him. I will never understand why he was allowed to come home to us in that state.

Writing this makes me sad all over again. I feel so sorry, not just for my young self and Peter, but for all who have suffered or are suffering the torment of mental illness. It could happen to anybody. Sometimes we don't see the signs and sometimes there aren't any.

mr postman

I have been writing to Dorothy for over sixty years now, ever since I left England. We were in school together and somehow we stayed in touch. Today, I still get letters from her, in spidery old lady writing, which she sends from her home in London. I have to get out my magnifying glass to read them. It takes me ages but, no matter, I have the time.

I have always loved to write letters. My daughter Rachael unearthed a bag of them recently. I wrote her newsy, gossipy letters and we laughed together as she read them to me. Yet another lockdown distraction. I remember when Rachael left home for good to go to Strathclyde University in Scotland to continue her studies. I can see her now with her bag in her hand on the doorstep, saying goodbye. I could have gone to the train with her, I could have made more of a fuss, but I didn't. I went back into the house and cried. I wrote and apologized to her, and her reply was wonderful.

. . . We were taught by you to survive and that's a great asset when you have no idea what you are letting yourself in for and no money in your pocket to speak of. I knew I would be ok whatever happened. So thank you for that. It's a weird feeling packing all your most precious things (luckily they fitted into one haversack!) and leaving such a safe environment with lots of activity and a comforting madness. Change is always hard but I suppose, the one thing I didn't know, and was sad about, was whether I would be missed or not.

She was missed all right. I just forgot to tell her.

Rachael didn't reply to my letters very often, so this one was special. She usually just picked up the telephone. I am so glad she kept my letters. They tell a story and they are tangible memories of what was going on with us all.

My memory plays tricks, but letters bring me back to special days, times and places. I took down the pink box from the top of my bookcase yesterday and I was transported by the letters my children had sent me from all over the place.

Peter wrote from London in August 1987, complaining about the long hours and the low pay at his job on the building site.

'I'm going to look for a rise,' he writes, 'and if I don't get it I'll give in my notice.' And, 'thanks for filling in my grant application form for college'.

I remember now I did a lot of that. They would all disappear to summer jobs abroad, leaving me with the complicated task of filling in those forms.

Sarah went to Italy as an au pair one summer in 1984. 'The sun is lovely here in Genoa and I have a million freckles,' she wrote.

Eddie wrote from America, 'People are very nice here. They seem to like me. I keep getting invited to cook-outs.' *Cook-outs – whatever are they?* I recall thinking at the time.

Brian wrote from Switzerland, New Zealand, Australia

and from his beloved India. He told me the story of his spiritual journey and said he hoped I would understand.

Michael wrote more than anyone else. He and I always had a good relationship despite his tendency to get himself into trouble. I remember the time I had gone to the pictures to see *Aliens*. I was still a bit shaky on the way back in the bus. It's a scary movie and I was alone. As I got home I was greeted with the news that Michael had been arrested.

When I had left the house earlier, Michael had just started his shift in Miss Roddy's shop on Sandymount Green. May Roddy had a little grocery store and stayed open late to oblige the customers. Most of my children had worked there to earn pocket money over the years. Miss Roddy's served freshly sliced ham and pink iced cakes. She had a chair in the shop where customers could sit while she sliced the ham and had a chat.

Michael had gone for his break and joined a couple of boys in the Green. There had been a few disturbances of late and the gardaí were checking out what the boys were doing. Michael had a penknife in his pocket. It had a wooden handle and a rusty blade, and the good men of the law put him into the back of the car and drove to Irishtown Garda Station where they charged him with having an offensive weapon.

When Michael was released and back at home we discussed what we should do. I immediately thought of

John. I had been doing some work for the local solicitor, John McKenna, and I knew he would help. He engaged a barrister. I would never have been able to afford that.

Michael was hoping to join his brother in America and might never get there if he received a criminal conviction. He was very angry with the way he had been treated over that knife. I was relieved it was a few weeks before we had to appear in court because by that time he had calmed down.

On the day, we got the bus into town and walked along the quays to the courthouse. It was packed with the good, the bad and the ugly of Dublin that morning. I was glad we had the barrister because it gave us an air of respectability. There were young men there that day who would be sent down because they had no one to speak up for them or simply because they lived at the wrong address.

After the barrister had said his piece, the judge called Michael to the stand and asked him if the knife was his and what he used it for. Michael explained that before he had gone into work he had been whittling a piece of wood to make a mould for a weight for his fishing rod.

'Where do you fish?' asked the judge.

'On the south wall, mostly, down by the red lighthouse,' Michael said.

'Do you catch much?'

'On good days a few mackerel.'

'You should try Dún Laoghaire pier,' the judge said. He looked down at the evidence in his hand, an old knife that had seen better days, and turned to the garda: 'You should be ashamed of yourself bringing such a charge to the court.'

And then he boomed: 'Case dismissed!'

Michael and I walked back along the quays, vindicated and jubilant. Suddenly he stopped. 'They didn't give me back my knife,' he said. Typical Michael, never satisfied. He had got out of a potential jail sentence or fine and all he could think about was the old knife.

Michael got his visa for America and went to work in San Francisco. His letters were great, telling me about the people and the boat he was living on. But there was one which was very special. I have it in my hand right now. It was written on stiff, light-blue paper. On the top it says *Monday, 13 November 1995, San Francisco.* I was so proud that Michael could share his feelings with me, and the ending . . . well, I was in tears.

Dearest Mother

I have fallen in love. She is the most wonderful girl I have ever met. When we are together I am overcome with joy and happiness. Her name is Bridget Brennan (Irish descent). She is twenty years of age, she is beautiful in every sense of the word. She is very intelligent and witty, very strong and most of all she is in love with me too.

Four weeks ago I was at one of those Sunday afternoon dance parties I told you about. This one was on a large boat that cruises around the bay. Towards the end of the evening, I was dancing away when I noted her. She too was dancing. She looked lovely, really happy. So I gave her some smiles. Soon after we began to dance together. We moved so well together and seemed to connect. After the music stopped, we chatted.

I found I liked this girl a lot. I asked could I see her again but to my dismay she told me that she had a boyfriend. However, she did give me her address and asked me to write her a letter. I told her that I had an Irish teacher called Miss Brennan in whose class I once got into trouble for writing a letter. So write I did.

Two weeks later at the last of the sunset parties of the year, I was dancing when I heard a voice calling my name. I turned and there was Bridget. The first line of the letter I had sent her were these: 'We shall dance again, maybe not floating to the rhythm of the tide, but floating, nonetheless'. So when I saw her I turned and said 'We shall dance again,' only to hear her sweet voice reply 'maybe not floating to the rhythm of the tide but floating nonetheless.' I think this might have been the most pleasurable moment of my life.

Since then we have been seeing each other regularly. She is a student in Berkeley in her third year of development studies and gets very high grades in all of her subjects. She has travelled to many places as her father often works overseas. They spent four years in Australia where she went to high school which I think has left her without many American issues.

Incidentally, her boyfriend broke up with her after our second encounter. I was glad to hear that news.

In the time that we have been together we have been intimate only once but did not fully make love. In January she is leaving for Mexico. She will be gone for six months doing research as part of her studies. Last night I asked her how she would feel about not making love until we were together again when she returns. I had momentarily amazed her. She paused and then told me she would love that.

She loves me for what I am. She appreciates my joy and free spiritedness and I love the way she sometimes in a nice way cuts me down to size (as you know that sometimes needs doing). It seems like we have always known each other. We share so much and see so many of the same things. She is very good and healthy. No cigarettes, no marijuana, just the rare glass of good red wine. She has extended my whole person, I love her.

However, there is another woman, just as important (actually much more so) that I am going to see soon. She also is beautiful and intelligent. I think you know who I am referring to!

Not long now, Mum,
Your always and ever loving son

Michael

I wanted to show it to everyone.

At that time, Gay Byrne on his radio show held a competition for people to send in letters from abroad. The prize was £500. I sent in this letter and, although I didn't expect to win, I hoped it would be read out. But Gay must have loved it. It won first prize and was read out on air in July 1996. Gay doubled the prize and we both received £500. I bought a three-piece leather suite from a friend who was downsizing and Michael settled his debts. Happy days.

Dear reader, the relationship did not flourish. Michael met a wonderful woman, Rukhsana, in London, and he is now married with two sons, Joseph and Lucas, and lives in Dublin.

I just don't understand why the others are always saying Michael is my favourite . . .

broken mind

Leaving Peter in St Brendan's was traumatic for both of us. I had to face people and answer their questions. They meant well. It seemed that everyone had seen the ambulance that night. What was I supposed to say? *My husband has gone mad. He thinks he's Jesus.*

The stigma was not just around Peter but the whole family. We were all tainted and Peter's illness could only be spoken of in whispers. There was a social stigma surrounding mental health issues at that time. I am not sure we have moved on that much even today. People experience panic attacks, depression, delusions, and you just can't see it. A broken leg, yes; a broken mind, no. Some people cannot accept behaviour that is classified as abnormal, out of their understanding, different. Things like cancer and heart conditions can be discussed openly and sympathy is always forthcoming. With mental illness, the shutters come down.

Now that I live on the northside of Dublin, I'm only a ten-minute walk away from what was once St Brendan's. It closed in 2013 and is now the city campus of the Technological University Dublin. In 1976, the nearest I had ever been to it was when I took the children to the zoo in Phoenix Park, two bus rides away from Sandymount.

The hospital, often simply known as Grangegorman, was built in 1814. In 1981, writing about his experiences of working there, psychiatrist Dr Michael Corry described St Brendan's as a 'custodial Dickensian workhouse':

I was stunned and changed by what I witnessed in the back wards of St Brendan's Hospital. The conditions were repulsive. The impact of seeing hundreds of unkempt human beings of all ages lying, sitting, and walking in smelly, shabby hallways and corridors, looking like inmates of a concentration camp, was staggering. This human zoo was caused by diffusion of authority, lack of accountability, lack of interest, conceptual gaps, the culture of silence, the inappropriateness of the medical model, involuntary detention . . .

And in his memoir, *Music and Madness*, Professor Ivor Browne described his first exposure to St Brendan's like this:

There were crowds of patients all jostling each other, some of the women with their dresses pulled up over their heads and here and there a nurse, struggling amid the chaos. There was a cacophony of sound and I felt as though I was lost in some kind of hell.

The consultant psychiatrist and former Inspector of Mental Hospitals Dr Dermot Walsh wrote that the large, impersonal wards in the hospital often housed more than a hundred patients each and very little was done for them in terms of rehabilitation.

I went in to see Peter every evening. 'We are waiting for you to get better and come home,' I told him. But he didn't believe there was anything wrong with him.

'Try to understand,' he would plead. 'I have been chosen.'

Peter remained delusional and normal conversation or interaction was impossible. I told him what the children were up to but he wasn't interested. He kept going back to his obsession. He was Jesus and nobody believed him.

One evening a letter appeared on the floor in the hall and it was from Peter. I was frightened that he had somehow got out of that dreadful place and was wandering around Dublin. I found out later that he had given the letter to someone visiting and they had put it through our letter box. The letter read:

Dear Ann

First of all I want to tell you I love you. What I wanted to do on Sunday was the truth that is to go and see my father, my son, my niece and myself and pray together in my father's house but no one would listen to me. I have the sacred heart and so has Tracy, who actually should have been called Mary, there are two sacred hearts. The devil got at me but he won't get at Tracy. The reason for being in here is to set these poor unfortunates free, all these sick people because I love them. The devil tricked me but he won't win because God is too good.

I would like, if possible, if I don't die in the next few days, to go and pray with them as I should have done before I went to St Dympna's and everyone would be better. The devil got at me but he forgot about the blessed virgin and he is afraid of her.

*I don't know if God is good enough to let me live but if not
I will be buried with my mother because I love her. She didn't
know what she gave birth to when I was born. I have sinned but
God told me to love everyone and I did.*

*I think the end of the world is going to come very shortly. It
will come quicker if I can go and pray with my father, our son
Eddie, and my niece. Don't think this letter is mad, it's not, it's
the truth. If it's possible to get out for just one hour to see them
I will show you the proof of what is to be.*

With all my love – protect Tracy for God's sake.

Peter

It was scary to see it all written down in black and
white in his own hand. I had been listening to it every
night when I went to see him but somehow this was
different.

It was hard to believe Peter would ever recover his sanity,
but, miraculously, as the days went by he began to return
to some kind of rational thinking. Whatever medication they were giving him had started to work. He had
been there for five weeks when a nurse informed me
one evening that he could go home the next day. I was
delighted. He seemed to have got over whatever was ail-
ing him and was anxious to get home.

I asked Peter's brother John to go and collect him in
his car. That turned out to be a big mistake. John just

wanted to get Peter – and himself – out of there as quickly as possible. He hadn't been in the sitting room when Peter was demented and wanted to kill us all. He didn't want to hear that. He didn't think there was anything wrong with Peter – or he didn't want to know if there was. So he went in and collected him without bothering to see a doctor, get a prescription of some kind or ask about his future care as an outpatient. He failed to ask the appropriate questions. But so did I. That was careless of me. I should have gone for Peter myself. I should have spoken to a doctor about what would happen next. In my ignorance, I didn't think.

I was so glad to have Peter home and away from St Brendan's. Nothing else mattered. He was lucid and no longer talking about religion, but part of him wasn't there. There was a vacant expression on his face as if he was looking for something and didn't know what it was. His hands and legs shook involuntarily at times but he seemed oblivious to it. It was difficult to get his attention for any length of time and when he talked his sentences trailed off into nothing. But he was home.

A few weeks went by and it was obvious he wasn't coping. I can see him now, sitting in the middle of the staircase, bewildered, gazing up at the still half-finished bathroom and talking about getting a job. Peter was trying desperately to stay with us and get on with life, but the effort was too much for him.

I did not understand that Peter's delusions had ceased

for the time being because of the medication he had received in St Brendan's. It kept him relatively sane for about three weeks and then the delusional obsessions started all over again. He began to go to Mass every day. He came back talking about God with an angelic smile on his face. He described the world to me through his eyes and what he saw and heard was beautiful.

One day Peter came home after one of his long walks and asked me to wash his feet. I tried to make excuses, but he was having none of it. He sat in the armchair calmly waiting for me to do as I was asked. There was a woman in the Bible who washed Christ's feet, he said. He omitted to say that, according to St Luke, she was a well-known sinner.

Peter rolled up his trousers, I knelt on the floor and washed his feet. The woman in the Bible did it with her tears and my tears too were dripping into the bowl of soapy water. *What harm*, I thought. It was little to ask, and it made him happy.

I couldn't find it in me to dismiss all Peter's strange and wonderful thoughts. How was I meant to disillusion him when he was so content in his private world? I kept trying to distract him with stupid talk. 'It's well for you, Peter,' I'd say, 'look at that pile of washing I have to do.'

I made him coddle for dinner, even though none of the rest of us liked it. Anything and everything to bring him back into the real world. Nothing worked.

Peter was not on any sick benefit so he still went to

the unemployment office every week. Back when he was drinking and backing the horses, I would try to get one of the children to go with him so that he would come straight home with the dole money. They loved it. He would stop off in O'Connell Street and buy them a Knickerbocker Glory in Cafolla's before getting on the no. 3 bus.

Now, it wasn't the money I worried about but Peter. I knew it wasn't right to take the children out of school but it was only once every five weeks. I alternated them.

It was Eddie's turn to accompany his father one day. As they were coming home, they passed the Star of the Sea Church where a hearse was parked outside. 'We must go in,' Peter told him.

Eddie walked behind his father down the centre of the church as Peter waved his arms and blessed the congregation. Peter extended his hands, praying loudly and incoherently when he reached the coffin. Eddie took his hand, gently turned him around and brought him home. I was told by those who were in the church that day that Eddie behaved with compassion and dignity. I wasn't surprised. I expected no less of the boy, then and now.

As the weeks went by the smiling stopped and Peter became frustrated. He couldn't get the delusions out of his mind and they were tormenting him. He wanted the voices and notions to disappear and give him peace. I could see in his face, in his constant rubbing of his head, that he was in agony. It was horrible to watch him as he tore at his hair in an effort to dislodge the constant pain.

'I want to die, I am no use to anyone,' he said, over and over. 'You would be better off without me.'

There was nothing I could do or say to console him. I knew that, if he could, he would take his own life. I couldn't let that happen.

Our local doctor saw the seriousness of the situation and referred us back to St Brendan's. Peter wasn't pleased. We sat in the taxi and, as we approached the hospital, he became agitated and begged me to take him home. But I couldn't. Peter, for the second time, bravely signed himself in to Grangegorman. And for the second time, feeling alone and useless, I left him there. My only hope was that this time they would be able to help his poor mind to come out of its torment.

smelling of scones

If you are related to me in any way, it might be best if you stop reading now. Look away, look away.

I love sex. Women don't talk about sexual pleasure very much, if at all. At least not in my circle. I tried to bring it up one time with friends who I meet for lunch and there was silence. We are all elderly widows and I just wanted to know if they missed it. Afterwards one of them said she always regarded it as a bit of a chore. She has five children. Each to their own. She loves playing golf.

During the last years of his life, Peter and I made love intermittently. The medication Peter was prescribed had taken its toll on his desire for sex. It was spasmodic and there was no chance that normal service would ever be resumed.

Each night as we lay together, it frustrated me that what had come so naturally all our married life was denied me, despite my best efforts. There was a time when I couldn't walk past the bed without being dragged in beside him, and I revelled in it. I had almost got used to doing without it when Peter was alive. I cuddled up to him in bed and that was enough. After he died, I didn't even have that.

So, when Harry called to ask me out for a drink I gratefully accepted. He was a friend of Peter's, ten years younger and the proverbial tall, dark and handsome type with a cheeky grin. When Harry was in trouble with the law, Peter had gone bail for him, putting up our house as collateral. Maybe he thought he owed me something.

I was a forty-one-year-old woman in the prime of her life sitting at that table drinking my gin and tonic. I wanted it. Sex. I didn't care how I came by it. I asked Harry to take me to the pictures and he agreed.

The pictures. A great euphemism.

We went into town on the no. 2 bus. The movie was *Kagemusha*, a Japanese sword-fighting epic. Harry had chosen it and was enjoying the killings on the screen. I focused on the heat of the man beside me as he casually put his arm around my shoulders. When we left the cinema, there was no need for words. He knew what I wanted and was only too happy to oblige.

Harry knew a bed-and-breakfast place in Summerhill that catered for this type of situation. Of course he did. He had obviously done this before. I had been with only one man for the past twenty years and I was nervous as we climbed the grimy stairs of that rundown boarding house.

Harry was a practised, energetic and efficient operator. He was doing his best but I kept saying, over and over again, 'You're doing it all wrong, you're doing it all wrong.' I had been so many years with Peter that I couldn't imagine there was more than one way to go about it. I didn't want there to be another way. I just wanted him to be Peter and he wasn't.

We got dressed. The buses had stopped running and we walked home on that cold winter night holding hands. I don't know what I expected from this experience, but

I didn't feel happy as we made our way along the Liffey. There was no love, no romance and no proper sex. How childish of me to expect otherwise.

Harry hummed 'Roxanne' as he brought me over the locks at Ringsend. It was dark, damp and a bit scary. The last time I had walked that way, it had been with Peter. But now everything looked different.

I had embarrassed myself. If I couldn't have Peter, what was the point?

I realized after this encounter that it wasn't just the sex. I wanted to prove that I was still attractive to a man. Looking in the mirror didn't tell me that. I needed someone to hold me, to love me and tell me all those things that women long to hear.

So I languished for a while, sexually anyway, and got on with being a widow woman with eight children, throwing myself into community work. It was my friend Pat who encouraged me to try again. A new pub had opened in Grand Canal Street, the Kitty O'Shea, and Pat said it was the place to go. It was crowded and, as we sat at the bar, two very acceptable men joined us. All was going well until my one said, 'You smell of scones.' He was probably more used to catching a whiff of Beautiful by Estée Lauder on the women he met. I had been baking for the Girl Guides cake sale all afternoon. But sometimes you go out smelling of Eau de Flour and reality comes crashing in.

Over time, I got the hang of this dating thing only to find that there are many duplicitous men out there. I was stood up on many occasions. 'I'll pick you up at eight,' he'd say and there I would be, all dressed up with nowhere to go. When a second date was arranged and he didn't show, I guessed that he was married. That night out had been a one-off while his wife was staying with her sister or mother or, worse, having a baby in the National Maternity Hospital.

One man with a warped sense of humour suggested we meet in The George on South Great George's Street. I didn't know until I entered it that The George was not meant for me. The drag queen sitting at the bar was a clue and I left hurriedly. That was unkind. I became even more cynical about men when on some occasions I went to a bar or a dance and saw husbands of women I knew. I had read *The Women's Room* by Marilyn French and my opinion of men has never quite recovered from that book and my experiences.

I often went off on my own to a literary event or one of those comedy clubs which had started up. I became more confident and comfortable going it alone. I struck gold on one of those occasions. I met a Swedish man who, aesthetically, was all that I could ever desire: blond hair, blue eyes and a Scandinavian tan. I had been to a lecture in Buswells Hotel, which had proved too boring for words. On the way home I called in to a pub in Haddington Road and that's where I met him. He was over here with his brother for a bridge tournament, of all things. He was much younger than me, although I don't think he realized that at the time. Both of them were great craic and they invited me back to their bridge-playing friend's house in Booterstown. When I said I had to leave, my new Swedish friend offered to walk with me. We arrived at my house in the early hours of the morning and what ensued in the front room was pure Carlsberg – probably the best sex of my life. I hadn't bothered to tell him that I had eight children. I am not sure what he thought when one by one the youngest members of the household came traipsing in to watch the early-morning shows on television. Fortunately, he was long gone before the others emerged from their beds that Saturday morning.

I didn't always have to go out to meet men – sometimes they just knocked on my door. G was one of those. Originally from Liverpool, he was an artist and a poet going door to door selling his wares. He told us that he had been to school with John Lennon. The older children were enthralled, and he became a regular visitor, often staying for something to eat. One night he called quite late, as I was making sandwiches for the school lunches. I offered him tea and he sat in the front room as I went to the kitchen. When I returned, tray in hand, he was sitting on the settee completely naked. It was a cold November night and we had no central heating at the time. Nothing occurred that evening. I didn't fancy him anyway.

*

I had several longer-term relationships, some of them with the most unlikely people. C comes to mind whenever I hear Marilyn Monroe singing about the hidden talents of an unpromising lover in the Irving Berlin classic 'You'd Be Surprised'. He was an eccentric and much loved by everyone who knew him. He had an encyclopaedic knowledge of popular music and all manner of things. Great man to have on your side in a pub quiz, but, oh, how he could talk. One evening we were going to O'Reilly's in Sandymount for a drink. We walked to the corner and C met some friends and stopped to chat. I said I would go on and get the drinks in. I drank my whiskey and dry ginger and looked at the pint of lager on the counter beside me. An hour later I left and there was C still at the corner, talking. Such a talkative man but lovely all the same.

I spent several years on and off with P. He loved fast cars and gold jewellery. He taught two of my children to drive and was a generous man. He became very ill and always says I saved his life. Really, it was the medics in St Vincent's and their recommendation that he should live in a warm climate.

He took a job at Paradise Beach on Mykonos, and he asked me to join him with my two youngest, Katie and Michael. I jumped at the chance. I took a sabbatical from work and we spent three months camping in the sunshine. I swam naked in the sea, Katie ate figs from the trees and Michael learned to scuba dive. It was idyllic for a while.

What's that old saying, if you want to know someone go and live with them? And you really get to know some-one when you're sharing a caravan on a beach in Paradise. I suppose the crunch came the night he jumped out of bed and grabbed his pitchfork. Some of the campers were making a noise and P was trying to sleep. He went out into the black night wildly stabbing with that dan-gerous implement. He could have killed someone. He lives in Spain now and calls me every year on my birth-day to tell me I am the love of his life.

J, yet another old friend of Peter's, came to call. They worked and lived together in Sheffield in their teens. He was a big-time philanderer and has no doubt lost track of all the women he's had in his life. Mathematics was never one of his strong suits. He caused me consider-able heartache over the years as he dropped in and out of my life. He rang me just last week, telling me of his undying love and asking me to marry him. He's eighty now and living on the top of a mountain in Tipperary.

In September 2003, the journalist daughter had to go to Lisdoonvarna to report on the annual matchmak-ing festival there. She brought me along as a guinea pig, I suppose. After speaking to Willie Daly, the resident matchmaker, I was instructed to meet up with a man at Doolin. He came highly recommended as an ideal match. I went there at the appointed time. The man arrived but he said he couldn't delay because he had to see about the 'kettle'. I was taken aback – surely making tea was not of more importance than this auspicious moment? Amid roars of laughter it was explained to me that it was the 'cattle' he was worried about.

I dropped the idea of a relationship with a farmer and looked further afield. I had always dreamed of going on a cruise and when I sold my house in Sandymount and had money to spare, I did just that. On my first night on the boat, I stayed up late listening to the piano man playing and singing. At the end of the evening, he came over and sat with me. He was interesting and great company and, like many a man before him, he told me the story of his life. After that, every evening when I walked into the lounge he would begin to play 'Annie's Song'. It was so romantic. We had to wait until we docked and could leave the boat before we got together. There were strict rules for cruise members. I see him now on Facebook from time to time.

You'd think after all that I would have ended up with someone. I suppose I didn't really need or want a replacement father for my children or a new husband. And despite what you might be thinking after reading all this, I love men, especially if they are interested in me and listen. I spent a whole weekend in Kerry once listening to a man tell me all about his life and he never once asked me any questions about mine.

My ideal man is someone who is curious and interested in me as a person. A man who enjoys sex and is attentive to my needs. A man who is not a bore and can make me laugh. And, sometimes, you just need a tall, blond Swedish man who plays bridge.

It was on my sixtieth birthday that a friend gave me an item she had bought for me at the Ann Summers shop in O'Connell Street. It proved useful over the years. About three years ago, I decided I didn't need it any more. The humour had gone off me. I wrapped it up in newspaper and put it into the bin at the bus stop. What else could I do with it? I know you are supposed to dispose of electrical or battery-operated items at a certain place at the waste disposal but I couldn't ask my housemates to do that for me.

My interest in sex gradually diminished in my late seventies and now, well, it's almost completely gone. But if I see Jeff Bridges or Mark Ruffalo on Netflix, it puts the longing on me.

shocking treatment

After my beautiful Peter signed himself in to St Brendan's for the second time it was four days before I was allowed to see him. I arrived on a sunny afternoon to find him sitting on a bench in the garden in one of the nicer parts of the hospital. I was happy to see him out of the ward and looking so peaceful. He was smiling again but in a strange way. I sat down beside him and held his hand.

Peter looked at me as if I was a stranger. He appeared to be in a state of euphoria and I almost envied him. He was talking about the birds, the singing of the birds. He wasn't imagining things this time: the birdsong in the quiet garden was beautiful.

'That's a blackbird,' he said and he started to sing.

If I were a blackbird, I'd whistle and sing . . .

Peter could identify the call of the blackbird and remember the words of the song, but he didn't know that his wife was sitting beside him. I asked him questions, but he barely answered. He just kept looking around as if he had never seen a flower or the sky before. He appeared to have no memory of how he got there or what had happened to him. It was obvious that he didn't care about anything at all. He was blissfully happy.

When I said goodbye, he scarcely acknowledged my leaving. He was like a lost soul, albeit a very happy one, with no connection to anybody, not even me.

I left him sitting there. I didn't know what to think. I assumed that he was on some special drug that seemed to be giving his poor tormented brain a rest. *That must be it*, I told myself. *It will all come right.* The delusions were not tormenting him and, even if Peter seemed to be away with the fairies now, he would come back. I tried to convince myself that this was only a temporary thing, but still I was confused and needed to talk to someone who could tell me what was going on.

The psychiatrist said that Peter had been given Electroconvulsive Therapy (ECT) very shortly after he was admitted because of his aggressive behaviour. 'He was violent and making threats. It was for the best,' I was told.

'Why didn't you let me know?' I said.

There was no need to let me know because, apparently, they were not obliged to do so. I never knew if Peter consented to the treatment or if he was in any condition to decide one way or another.

'What have you done to him? He doesn't know me any more.' I was in tears by now, but that doctor must have seen distressed wives crying about their husbands many times before.

He remained calm as he told me in his clinical language that ECT was a procedure in which electric currents are passed through the brain, intentionally triggering a brief seizure. One of the side effects is loss of memory, he said. He could see by my face I was horrified.

'Don't worry,' he said. 'He will regain his memory and return to normal very soon.'

Normal, after having an electric current coursing through his body? I found that extremely hard to believe.

My next question was would the ECT cure his obsessional, deranged thinking, but the doctor was non-committal.

'So why was it necessary then?' I asked. 'Why did he have to have the ECT if it wasn't going to help his condition?'

He told me that they had no alternative but to give him the treatment because he had become violent and was suicidal. 'We will wait and see how he comes along. The memory loss is temporary,' he said, 'you'll see.'

Although I got a hold of myself and stopped crying, I was angry. No, I didn't see, and now I know I wasn't alone. Greater minds than mine agree that ECT was not necessarily the answer. Dr Peter Breggin, a Harvard-trained psychiatrist and one of the world's leading critics of ECT, wrote in 1997:

> In the case of ECT, a large percentage of people are being harmed, and there's little evidence that many are helped. There's no evidence that the treatment prevents suicide or rescues desperate cases. At best the treatment offers a very poor trade-off: potentially irreversible brain damage and mental dysfunction in exchange for docility and temporary emotional blunting or euphoria that results from the damage.

Euphoric and docile, that's how Peter was that day.

However, medicine moves on. Nowadays, a modified version of ECT is used to great effect for people in severe stages of depression but only after all other medication has failed. Every year approximately 250 people receive the treatment in Ireland. Writing in the *Irish Medical Times* in March 2019, Dr Dermot Ward said:

> ECT is indeed one of the finest treatments in the whole of medicine. Would we belittle an antibiotic which cured a severe pneumonia because that patient might or might not have a recurrence of that illness? I have known patients profoundly depressed who received ECT more than thirty years earlier and still no recurrence. If a patient gets four or eight years complete relief following a course of ECT for an acute mental illness, and it recurs perhaps eight years later and ECT is again successful, then that is truly remarkable. Especially when it is more than likely antidepressant medication would have been prescribed without any or adequate effect.

On that sunny day in St Brendan's there were more revelations to come. In my innocence, I asked the doctor if Peter would be going back to St Dympna's for more treatment. He smiled and replied in a patronizing tone, 'He's not an alcoholic, he has been diagnosed with schizophrenia.'

Schizophrenia. Wasn't that the disease where people had two different personalities? I didn't actually know what the word meant and the doctor did not have the time nor inclination to enlighten me. I left the hospital with all this new information about Peter's illness but none of it made sense to me. I had to do my research.

You will probably be amazed to know that we owned an edition of the *Encyclopaedia Britannica*, all thirty-two volumes – big, brown, faux-leather-covered hardbacks. Peter had answered the door to a salesman on one of his more lucid days and was taken with the idea. We already owned the one-volume *Pears' Cyclopaedia* and, along with *Brewer's Dictionary of Phrase and Fable*, I thought that was sufficient. When the children saw the book the man pulled out for his demonstration, it was all 'Please say yes, Mum.'

'Pay by the month,' the man told us.[1]

I went to the encyclopaedia and under 'S' found the symptoms of schizophrenia: hallucinations, delusions, blunted emotions, disordered thinking and a withdrawal from reality. That sounded about right and now I had a name for what was wrong with Peter. It was a start. After

---

1. I paid those instalments, along with all the other bills, until Peter died, whereupon we were informed of a clause in that contract which said if the buyer deceased the books would be ours with no further payments necessary. So, Peter died and bequeathed us the *Encyclopaedia Britannica*.

more research, I discovered that there was a relatively new organization, the Schizophrenia Society of Ireland,[2] and I contacted them. I attended meetings in Newtownpark Avenue in Blackrock, bought a duplicated leaflet for 15p and learned more.

Schizophrenia is an illness that usually starts in or soon after adolescence. Peter's was the paranoid type that often comes to people after thirty. I was told about the rule of thirds: one third of those diagnosed would recover completely; a further third would improve over time, leaving the remaining third who would not show any improvement.

Gradually the effect of the ECT wore off and Peter began to regain his memory. How much, I will never know, but at least he knew who I was.

When the time came for his discharge from hospital, I went to collect him. He was referred to a clinic in Ballsbridge as an outpatient for injections of Anatensol Decanoate, otherwise known as Fluphenazine, an antipsychotic medication that was administered every fortnight. The effects of those injections were horrendous. Peter sat in the chair rotating his ankle for hours on end, rarely spoke and had no interest in anything around him. It was terrible to watch him in this pathetic state. Now, not only did the children have an unemployed

---

2. Now Shine – www.shine.ie.

father, they had to cope with this person who sat, uncomprehending, in a chair all day.

Peter took up smoking in hospital. He came home with a packet of Sweet Afton in his pocket and a box of matches. He had never smoked before. I had given it up after Michael was born, but when I used to smoke Peter complained and encouraged me to stop.

Peter stayed in bed for hours, often not getting up until after midday. When he did manage to get out of bed he sat in his chair smoking, staring into space and fidgeting. His fingers were brown from the nicotine. He sat puffing away, not letting go of the cigarette until there was nothing left. As he stared into space, the children moved around him. They were uncomfortable in his presence. They didn't bring home friends any more. They were too embarrassed and didn't want people to see their father in this condition.

When Peter did speak, it was always about the same thing: taking his own life. He even asked me to help him. I told him that he would get better in time, although I hardly believed it myself.

'You'd be better off without me,' rang in my ears day after day.

The injections, the ECT, none of it had worked. Peter was still suffering and I could do nothing for him.

under one roof

Don't ask me to run up the stairs, I can't do that any more. As for pushing the vacuum around the place, forget it. I wouldn't venture up a stepladder to hang a picture or struggle for something on the top shelf. But I don't have to do any of those things because I live with Katie and Killian.

I don't know of anyone living an intergenerational life except us. Intergenerational or multigenerational living is where three generations of one family live together. This was commonplace in the last century and remains so in many developing parts of the world. I asked my son-in-law this morning if any of his friends are doing it. 'No,' he said as he walked out of the door to his upstairs stay-at-home office with his first coffee of the day in his hand, 'they've got more sense.' I think he was joking.

I live in a ground-floor room of a house in Phibsboro with my youngest daughter, Katie, her husband, Killian, and their three children, Síofra, Iseult and Mícheál.

After I sold the family home in 1999,[1] I rented a two-bedroom apartment in Windmill Lane in Dublin's city centre. Ten years later, Katie and Killian were living together in a one-bed flat and paying an exorbitant

---

1. I sold it to a plastic surgeon who has his practice there now. He was only interested in whether I was leaving the garden shed for his workmen to put their tools in. He demolished the house completely and rebuilt with an extra storey.

rent. They asked if they could move into my spare room and share the rent. They were saving for a deposit on a house and they moved in with me in 2009 and married the next year.

When Katie became pregnant, they decided it was time to move to more spacious accommodation. I don't remember too much discussion about whether I would go with them. They came up with the idea and maybe at the time we didn't think of it being forever. We had got on well so far and it suited us all.

Of course, it wouldn't have worked if my relationship with my son-in-law, Killian, was not good. There was none of that mother-in-law syndrome, beloved of old-time comedians. For my part, I understand completely why Katie fell for him. He is an intelligent, straightforward, decent man from Cashel. I always wanted relations in the country. Besides that, Killian is my tech support, solving any problems that arise with my computer or the internet.

We moved together three times until 2014 and two children later, when they bought the house in Phibsboro. The front room is my designated area and I have my own shower room and toilet under the stairs. I never go upstairs, no need. We share the kitchen and sitting room, in which Mícheál was born in May 2018. (All of Katie's children have been born at home. It has been my privilege and joy to be close at hand after each birth.)

*

When I sold the family home in Sandymount, I couldn't take everything with me. My neighbour Valdi offered to mind my things until I got sorted with a place. The weeks turned into months and she had to call me in the end to find out what I was going to do about my belongings. I had lived for three months without them and it hadn't cost me a thought. That taught me an important lesson.

I have dispensed with many of my belongings. That was not too difficult because, as I moved, things just dropped off. Now, everything I own is in my room. When I go, my family will be spared the ordeal of disposing of an accumulation of useless objects.

I have had to give away hundreds of books but as my eyesight has deteriorated that was only sensible. I love the books I have left and often take one or other down and squint at it with my reading glasses by the light of my extra-bright reading lamp. I have collected many volumes of poetry over the years and it is to those books that I turn, ragged and falling to pieces as they are. Today I picked up *Poems of Pleasure* by the American Ella Wheeler Wilcox and read a century-old poem, 'Now'. Somehow, it speaks to me:

> One looks behind him to some vanished time
> And says, 'Ah, I was happy then, alack!
> I did not know it was my life's best prime –
> Oh, if I could go back!'

Another looks, with eager eyes aglow,
  To some glad day of joy that yet will dawn,
And sighs, 'I shall be happy then, I know.
  Oh, let me hurry on.'

But I – I look out on my fair today;
  I clasp it close and kiss its radiant brow,
Here with the perfect present let me stay,
  For I am happy now.

I bought all the furnishings for my room along with a beautiful red fitted carpet. I have a bookcase with a shelf for my ornaments. I have a wardrobe, a bed, a bedside cabinet, an armchair and a huge television that acts as the monitor for my computer. I have a very smart desk, a comfortable typing chair and a laundry basket. My dirty washing goes into that and, miraculously, clean clothes, neatly folded, are handed back.

On the top of my wardrobe is a suitcase full of photographs and scrapbooks. On the top of my bookcase are two boxes containing my life. I had to get them down and dust them off as I began to write this book. Boxes of memories. School reports, letters, newspaper clippings, forms and instructions about my death.

My window looks out on to the street and my window box sits on the sill. I look after it. As I write, it is resplendent with cyclamen and I can see the tiny heads of snowdrops emerging. I bought a large trough from

Mr Middleton, the garden shop in Mary Street, last year, but it got in the way in our tiny back garden. It was moved to the front and now I have another outlet for my horticultural endeavours. Just as well, because Katie and I have been known to fall out about what should go where in the garden. She has green fingers and the house is full of plants.

There are three small trees in the garden, which were planted to mark the birth of the children. An apple tree for Síofra, a cherry tree for Mícheál and a plum tree for Iseult. Each year I make plum jam, pots of it. That's one very important contribution I make to the household and I love doing it.

When my door is open it's a sign that I am happy to see everybody. When it's closed everyone knows I am busy with one thing or another, whether it's sleeping, dressing, doing the crossword or writing. Nobody comes in without knocking. The youngest grandchild, three-year-old Mícheál, knocks and knocks. He knows the story but, instead of ignoring him, I find myself opening the door no matter what I am doing. He comes to me when it's time for dinner and takes me by the hand to lead me to the kitchen.

We eat dinner together. Breakfast and lunch, I look after myself. We share the cooking mostly, although since my shoulder injury I tend to do less than my fair share. Generally, though, we take it in turns. 'We eat well in this house,' Killian says, and he's right. Everyone has their own style and preferences. I tend to cook the old-fashioned food, like lamb stew with dumplings or bacon and cabbage. With parsley sauce, of course. Katie does a great aubergine parmigiana with gnocchi on the side and we all love Killian's teriyaki salmon. It is lucky we have the same taste in food (except for coriander: I hate it).

After dinner, I usually watch *In the Night Garden* on the television with Mícheál and then retire to my room. Generally, we don't see one another until the next day.

As well as food, my heating, lighting, Wi-Fi, Netflix and Spotify are covered by the rent I pay. Not sure if 'rent' is the right word, more a contribution to the general running of the household.

Katie is a great one for local freecycle groups and all sorts of things come into the house and many go out as quickly. When I had the bad shoulder, Katie sourced one of those chairs you can sleep in. I used it for six weeks and then it went back on the freecycle for some other injured soldier.

Material things are essential, of course, and I appreciate them. But more important to me is the love that comes seeping under my door. I love children, my own grandchildren in particular. Síofra explains how you can carry tens when you're adding, and I pretend to be amazed at this discovery. Iseult asks to use my mobile phone to watch YouTube: 'Don't worry, Nanny, it's kids' stuff, not adult.' Both of them ask if they can do anything for me, if I need anything. 'Shall I make your bed, Nanny?'

And all those cuddles that kept me going through the Covid-19 lockdowns were wonderful. When those children get older, and the kissing and cuddling diminishes, I might get a dog.

Grandmothers are notorious for 'spoiling' children. What nonsense, it's our prerogative. But I do have to watch my step and try not to interfere when it comes to parenting. There are so many things to think about these days that never occurred to me when I was raising my family. Using the pronouns 'he' or 'she', for example.

'Not all nurses are women, not all doctors are men,' Katie reminds me. 'It's not your fault, it's the patriarchy,' she says.

Pink and blue, trucks and dolls, and gender stereotyping were things I never gave much thought. The only thing I was adamant about was never letting my children play with guns. Even so, the boys – yes, it was always the boys – would make them from bits of stick.

So, I try not to interfere, and I like to think that most of the time I succeed. But it's not all sunshine and buttercups. Sometimes Katie and I have heated discussions. Killian looks on in dismay, wondering how the woman who does her mother's washing, vacuums her room and cuts her toenails can argue with that mother so vehemently. And why that same mother, who is always so grateful, retaliates. When serious disagreements arise, they are quickly remedied with a 'sorry' and a quick hug. We never go to sleep on it.

If I sense a difference of opinion arising between my daughter and her husband, I discreetly disappear. Much as I would love to stay and listen, put my oar in, do a bit of marriage counselling, I restrain myself and leave.

My housemates go to Cashel for a weekend now and again. 'Free gaff, Mum,' Katie says as she waves good-bye. And for the first few hours, I love it. Just the first few hours. I potter, go to the pictures in the afternoon and come home to an empty house. I love hearing the car drawing up to the door on Sunday evening.

I go away on holiday quite often too and I like to think I am missed. I can never spend Christmas Day at home. It wouldn't be fair to the rest of the family; Katie and Killian have me all the year round.

Tolerance is an essential part of communal living. I am sure there are many of my little idiosyncrasies that annoy my housemates. They try to ignore them as I do theirs. It's the only way. I get a little aggravated by their constant, 'Have you drunk your water?', 'When are you going out for that walk?', 'Have you done your exer-cises?' But it's a small price to pay.

I am happy living here with Katie. There are advan-tages for the rest of my children too. They know that someone is keeping an eye on me. That's what you have to do with old people, isn't it – keep an eye on them? We might do all sorts of mad things if you didn't.

My ninety-three-year-old sister emailed me yesterday saying that she was having a new shower installed and complaining that her children won't let her have a bath any more. 'It comes to something,' she said, 'when your children tell you what you can and can't do.'

For me, the way I live is ideal. Some of my friends say they would hate to give up their cosy lives and move in with one of their children. Another says that none of them would have her anyway. Many of them are rat-tling around in three-bedroom houses quite happily and fiercely guarding their independence. They say that liv-ing alone gives you the option to do whatever you want, when you want, with no constraints. The trouble is, as you get older, there are some things you can no longer do and others that just don't interest you any more.

I have gained so much from being part of this inte-grated way of living and I don't feel as if I have lost anything, least of all my independence. I have a happy and fulfilled life surrounded by people who love me.

The day may come when I will be a burden to my housemates. I hope I will accept that gracefully and move on. Meanwhile, for now, I have respect and privacy along with love and care. That's enough for any old woman.

pandemic

I read an article on the internet in February 2020 and, without checking on the author's scientific credentials or his ability to read a crystal ball, I fell for it. I wanted to believe that in seventy-five days all would be well. I needed that hope. In his article he said the following:

> The pandemic period is around seventy-five days. In the first three weeks, the number of cases increases exponentially, in the next three weeks, the number of new cases per day plateaus and in the final three weeks, the number of new cases drops exponentially. If my calculations are correct, the pandemic will be over by the end of April and theoretically, all bans could be lifted . . .

Don't judge me. I'm an optimist.

I started my hundred-day diary, giving a twenty-five-day leeway to ensure that the end would definitely be in sight by then. I won't bore you with all 30,000 words of it, just the following three entries.

Thursday 26 March – Day 14

Right now, I feel like an angry child. I will not go for my walk. I will not read the papers any more, nor will I go on Twitter. I am sulking. I was in denial first of all, imagining that as we are on an island any impact would be minimal. Then I decided that if I do everything I am asked it will go away. Now I am in a state of despair because I can only see weeks and weeks of this and I don't feel I can cope. I am one of the lucky

ones but I feel so desperately sad that I can barely function. Today is not a good day and it is only 10.30 in the
morning.

Killian is making lasagne for the dinner tonight.

Tuesday 26 May – Day 75
This is the day when he said it would be all over and
whilst it is true that nobody died yesterday and there
were only fifty new cases, we are not quite there. Made
a meat pie, well, two actually, roast squash, green beans
and new potatoes. The pie was delicious. New cases
today down to thirty-seven.

Saturday 20 June – Day 99
I walked to the North Strand today along the canal.
It takes me 45 minutes and 5,000 steps. It was great to
be out and visiting. Katie made her lovely broccoli and
beef dish for dinner.

Reading through that diary is depressing. The one
consistent and continual theme is food. It became so
important to know what was for dinner, who would
be cooking it and when we could eat it. On Twitter are
photographs of other people's dinners complete with a
complementary glass of wine on show. This doesn't help
as some of them looked very upmarket compared to my
shepherd's pie. Usually, we only have wine at the week-
ends, but in lockdown there was wine with everything,

even egg and chips. I saw on Twitter today someone writing that they had put on ten years since Covid. I felt like responding: *Me too, ten years and ten pounds.*

I miss my little trips to town on the bus for a bento box in Ukiyo or a blaa in Hatch & Sons. I rarely eat out in the evening but love my morning outings for lunch or a movie at the Irish Film Institute in Temple Bar.

There were some rays of sunshine and the Abbey Theatre's production *Dear Ireland* was one. It was a series of fifty specially written monologues exploring life during the Covid-19 crisis. It was a wonderful experience to sit watching from the comfort of my armchair.

As I get older, I find it hard to get going in the evening to go to the theatre. I mostly stick to matinees. So it was a treat to watch plays without having to go outside the door. The National Theatre in London put on a play every week and I watched all of them. I changed my mind about James Corden – he was quite brilliant in *One Man, Two Guvnors*. It was a privilege to be able to watch *Small Island*, adapted from the great book of the same title by Andrea Levy. It took me back to London after the war and the terrible racism endured by so many.

During the first lockdown, there was plenty of new entertainment to look at and explore. We are all jaded now and in the third lockdown there are not so many things to look forward to. I've watched television, Netflix and whatever else I could get my hands and eyes on. I wanted to buy things on Amazon but there was nothing I needed that could be bought there. My hair grew and so did a few hairs on my chin, which I usually get seen to every month in the local beauty salon. It didn't seem to matter any more. I've stopped looking in the mirror.

Telephoning friends regularly became a habit. They had little to say because, just like me, nothing much was happening in their lives. My friend June, who always buys the *Radio Times* and the *RTÉ Guide*, kept me informed of anything worthwhile to watch on television or listen to on the radio.

I knitted and did crosswords. Before being locked down, I had never been able to finish the *Irish Times* cryptic crossword. Well, I never tried too hard. If I couldn't manage the first two clues quickly, I abandoned the effort and did the Simplex instead. But, with all the time in the world, I persisted and can finish the cryptic most days easily. Crosaire in the *Irish Times*, yes, but the *Guardian* one still eludes me.

I hadn't knitted for years and taking up the needles was tricky. If I dropped a stitch and couldn't see well enough to pick it up, I unravelled it, yards of it. It didn't matter, I have all the time in the world. Every little bit of wool in the house was used and I begged some from friends. I took to buying wool online from This is Knit and even ventured into the shop one day when restrictions were lifted. I made the most ridiculous multicoloured scarfs that went on forever. Too long even for Dr Who.

Many scarfs later, I started on hats, thanks to instructions my then ninety-two-year-old sister sent by email. She, like my mother, is an excellent knitter. She has a knitting machine now. Joyce is so proficient that she can watch old black-and-white movies on DVD while at the same time knitting jumpers galore for her grandchildren and great-grandchildren.

I knitted dozens of those hats in many different sizes and gave them as Christmas presents. I am not sure how many of them are currently on their heads, but I did see my eldest grandchild, Fionn, wearing his when he called the other day to wave at me through the window. Now, in this third lockdown, I am on to fingerless gloves. I made up the pattern myself. Let me know if you want instructions.

I had one unbelievably bad day during that first lockdown. Well, many, actually, but this one stands out. I couldn't complete the crossword and the man from Poetry Ireland hadn't phoned. I had received a call the day before asking would I like a poem read to me. I was enchanted by the idea and when 10.30 came and went and the call hadn't come, I felt let down. I had coffee with Katie and she could see how fed up I was.

'Why don't you ring SeniorLine?' she suggested when her own words of comfort didn't seem to be doing it.

I looked them up and read that, 'SeniorLine is a national confidential listening service for older people provided by trained older volunteers.' The writing on their website was small and faint, which seems strange considering it is for older people like me.[1] Anyway, the woman at the end of the line was most sympathetic. Sympathy was just what I needed at that moment.

I told her that not being able to go for a walk was frustrating me.

I told her about the man from Poetry Ireland.

I wittered on for ages and she made all the right noises. And then she asked if I had a subscription to the *Irish Times*, which I thought was an odd thing to ask.

'Yes, I have,' I said.

'There is a woman working on that paper called Róisín Ingle who is writing articles that might be good for you at this time.'

I couldn't answer for a moment.

'She's my daughter,' I finally said. Upon which the woman started to tell me how great she was, how she loved her writing, how I should be so proud, and did I know how Queenie was doing.

I immediately telephoned Róisín and told her the story. It cheered us both up and we had a laugh. Of

---

1. I pressed the Control and + keys to make everything bigger. You might not know that, so I am throwing it out there in case your eyes are giving you trouble.

course, she put it in her column two days later. She's always at that, writing about me and her mother-in-law-in-waiting, Iris – better known as Queenie. People often ask me if I mind it when she writes about me. I don't. And Iris loves it. There are many more copies of the *Irish Times* purchased in Portadown on the days she gets a mention. (What I do dislike is when people introduce me as 'Róisín Ingle's mother', though it's a compliment in one way, I suppose. I believe her partner, Jonny, has to put up with a similar problem.)

Paddy Bushe, the Poetry Ireland man, eventually got through to me and read 'Cutting Grass' by Philip Larkin and then one of his own poems written during his isolation. It brought tears to my eyes.

The Etymology of Isolation

No man is an island, entire of itself – John Donne

I

Outside our window, above the wind-flecked
Bay between its two enclosing headlands,
A dozen gannets circle, now and then plunging
And struggling up to wheel and plunge again.
I am contemplating *isolation*, its meanings
In the here and now and then and again,
Contemplating that *isolate* shares its Latin
Island roots with *insulate*, that each one is also
A peece of the Continent, a part of the maine.
Isolation warms itself towards insulation.

II
I think of our son, whose house on the small
Peninsula across the bay I can just make out,
And who drops food and news and comfort
To our insulated door, like a boatman judging
A quick now or never surge to a storm-isolated
Island slipway, quickly heaving up supplies
One-handed, the other on the tiller steering
A curve astern. He smiles, waves. Half-joking,
Wholly grateful in this semi-isolation, I offer
A coinage: *peninsulated*. We'll live with that.

For me, Paddy's poem epitomizes all the kindness of sons and daughters throughout Ireland during this time, my own included.

I listened to poetry and many books as I knitted. I got through a couple of Anthony Trollopes, a few Iris Murdochs and *Zorba*.

Zorba the Greek, by Nikos Kazantzakis, is a book that I took out of the library when I was seventeen. When I showed it to my brother Ron, who like me was a great reader, he shook his head and said, 'You won't understand,' or some such patronizing remark. But he was wrong, I did understand and have read it many times since; so many insights, so many lessons. During those first few months of this awfulness I found it on Audible. There is a passage that gave me the hope I was looking for. That man on the internet who had me believing it was going to be over in seventy-five days failed me. I have transcribed Zorba's words, which I listened to on my walks along the canal. It is all I have by way of solace. It gives me strength.

When everything goes wrong, what a joy to test your soul and see if it has endurance and courage! An invisible and all-powerful enemy – some call him God, others the Devil, seems to rush upon us to destroy us; but we are not destroyed[. . .]

One night on a snow-covered Macedonian mountain a terrible wind arose. It shook the little hut where I had sheltered and tried to tip it over. But I had shored it up and strengthened it. I was sitting alone by the fire, laughing at and taunting the wind. 'You won't get into my little hut, brother! I shan't open the door to you. You won't put my fire out; you won't tip my hut over!'

My little hut is still standing; I hope yours is too.

way out

Peter continually thought about taking his own life. It was always there. 'You are better off without me' became his mantra. He felt it was his only way out. I did all I could to talk him around. I told him that he had so much to look forward to. The children would grow up to do great things, I told him. 'You will get better,' I said in an attempt to convince the both of us.

The man who could captivate an audience in Nolan's on a Sunday evening was gone. Peter, before his illness, would silence a pub full of rowdy drinkers. He sang 'My Boy Bill', the eight-minute soliloquy from *Carousel*, and still held their attention. If someone asked him for a song that he didn't know, he would learn it. The next week he would return to sing it to them, word and note perfect.

Peter used to tell me all about it when he came home on those Sunday evenings. He would be back in time for us to watch *The Onedin Line* together on the television. We loved that show. I heard the theme tune played the other day on the radio and the memories came flowing back along with the tears. I had to stop my knitting.

Peter remembered the man he once was, despite the ECT, and he could not tolerate what he had become. It was hard enough for me to look at him in pain but, for him, living it was a nightmare. He had gone from a vibrant, fun-loving, irresponsible man to this excuse for a person.

I was helpless. I telephoned and tried to speak to

someone in the out-patient clinic, but they were too busy. 'Make an appointment,' they said.

In desperation I wrote to Dr McCarthy, the doctor in charge of Peter's treatment at the out-patient clinic.

Dear Dr McCarthy

As Peter has been receiving treatment now for over six months I thought that the time was right to call in to have a chat about his condition and progress. I want to clear up a few things which I have in my mind about his illness and so I hope you will be able to help me.

It has occurred to me that doctors of psychiatry in trying to assess their patients are handicapped by not knowing them before their sickness. It is for this reason that I want to tell you something about Peter before his illness. He was a very happy go lucky person who found it very difficult to discipline himself and for this reason was unreliable and unable to face up to his responsibilities. He never really liked work but got on rather better with his workmates than those above him. Socially he was what one might term a 'charmer' but not of the wolfish variety. He is a great singer and this was his way of receiving free drinks as he entertained those around him. Of course when he was drinking he had the usual habits of excessive drinkers.

When we look at Peter now we see a very different person and some of the differences I must say I like very much. He is no longer unreliable, on the contrary I can nearly always depend on him. He is most undemanding and understanding of the day-to-day difficulties I have to face. On the other hand he has lost all joy in living and finds little point in doing anything much at all.

I understand that his stiffness and need to move some part of his body nearly all the time is due to his medication but does this consistent note of despondency also come from the treatment or from something else? He feels that his life has no point and isn't worth living. Can you do anything to make him feel differently? I have tried but do not seem to have succeeded.

I would like very much to be told the absolute truth as far as you can be expected to know it about Peter's condition. Will he, for example, be dependent on the injections forever and have to cope with the side effects? Will there ever come a time when he does not need injections and can resume a more normal life? Please do not misunderstand me. I am grateful for my husband's return to relative sanity, but I am at the same time concerned with his quality of life.

I am, of course, also concerned for myself and my family as it can be very hard to live with someone who cannot be enthusiastic about anything that is going on around him. Peter is also convinced that his mind is damaged. Is he right in thinking this or will all this living at 'low key' gradually give his brain a chance to right itself over a period of years. I want to know where we stand as I feel I can cope with knowing but it's the unsureness of the situation which is getting me down.

Regarding the question of work, I have tried different ways of getting him to do something in the house and garden but to no avail. The only time he does anything is when his brother, Nago, comes here and starts doing something for me and then

*he will work alongside him. His reflexes are very slow and his
initiative nil. I can't see him being able to hold down a job even
as a labourer but I do not, of course, say this to him but give
him every encouragement to try and find work.*

*Well now I have poured my thoughts into your sympathetic
ear and perhaps you can come up with some answers for me.*

*Yours sincerely
Ann Ingle*

I was so naive, so in awe of the doctors and their rem-
edies. How I could have imagined that my words would
make any difference to that overworked doctor who was
only doing her best is beyond me. But it was all I could
think of doing. I felt powerless and frustrated at my
inability to put things right, to make Peter happy again.

It was heart-breaking to see Peter like an old man, stiff
and lethargic all the time. As far as I was concerned, his
treatment was not curing him, it was turning him into a
zombie. I went with him to the clinic where he got those
injections one day. An air of hopelessness pervaded the
place. I saw all the other poor people who were going
through the same procedure. Everyone was being dosed
in order that they would remain free of their delusions
or psychotic behaviour and stay alive no matter what.
Staying alive, but at what cost?

In any case, for Peter it didn't work because in March

1978 he attempted to take his own life for the second time. Throwing himself at the fireplace was purposeful but not premeditated. This time he had worked it out.

Peter was still able to collect his social welfare each week and attend the clinic every fortnight, but apart from that he seldom left the house. One afternoon when Eddie came home from school Peter asked him to walk with him to his parents' house in Margaret Place. Peter went to ask his father for forgiveness, Eddie told me when he came back. I thought little of it because I was by now immune to Peter's strange behaviour. We all were.

The next day, he said he was going out for a walk. I didn't think too much about it and I was just glad that he was getting out of the house. It would do him good, I thought. When the children came home from school and he still hadn't returned, I sent Brian and Eddie out to look for him. They came back home for their dinner without their father. I was glad that they were not the ones to find him on the Strand.

As it started to get dark, a garda came to the door with the news that Peter was in hospital. He couldn't tell me any more. I ran all the way and arrived at St Vincent's panting and out of breath.

Peter had taken a knife, a bottle of whiskey and pain-killers with him on his walk to Sandymount Strand. He didn't go there to drown himself. He knew he couldn't drown there, you would have to walk to Wales to do that. But it was here he had chosen to end his life. It was somewhere precious to him and maybe he thought it a fitting place to die.

Peter had been found unconscious on the beach with his empty bottle of Powers beside him. The gardaí were called and he was taken to St Vincent's Hospital. The doctors pumped his stomach and managed to save his life. That wasn't what he wanted.

I was grateful that he was still in this world, no matter what. I loved him, you see, and selfish as it might sound, I wanted him with me. I knew his life was unbearable. But still I wanted him to live.

Peter was lying there on the hospital bed asleep. He looked like an old man; his face and hair were grey. He was dressed in a white hospital shift and looked like a corpse. I wanted to stay with him until he woke, but I was told to go. 'There is no point staying here,' they said. 'There is nothing you can do for him.'

I knew he would want me to be there when he woke up, but the nurse insisted. 'Come back in the morning,' she said.

I walked home in the rain.

Next morning, Peter was conscious but barely able to talk to me. I sat by his side and tried to make him eat the toast and tea the nurse had given him. I was glad he was there, not far from home and being looked after. The doctor arrived. I thanked him for saving Peter's life and he seemed embarrassed. 'Thank you,' I said again. 'How long will he have to stay here?'

'He can't stay here,' the doctor said abruptly.

What he said and the way he said it was strange, almost hostile.

'I've brought him clean clothes. I can get a taxi and take him home right now,' I said. I didn't appreciate the way that doctor was speaking to me. I was beginning to get annoyed with his attitude.

'That's not possible. He has to go to St Brendan's,' the doctor said. 'The ambulance will be here shortly.' He didn't look at me directly.

It was weird. It felt as if they wanted rid of us as soon as they possibly could. There was something going on that I didn't understand. It was sometime later that I realized what it was.

What the doctor was avoiding saying was that the gardaí could have been called and Peter might have been charged with an offence. At that time, attempting to take one's own life was against the law. The relevant legislation dated back to 1871 and stated:

> Where any person is charged before a justice of the district with having in any manner attempted to commit suicide, if the person charged shall confess the same, it shall be lawful for the justice to convict the person charged, and commit him to the common gaol or house of correction, there to be imprisoned, with or without hard labour, for any period not exceeding three months . . .

Legally, a person attempting to take their own life had to be jailed. In practice, the law was fudged. The way out was to lock these people away in a lunatic asylum and, in some cases, throw away the key. Suicide was decriminalized in Ireland in 1993; in many parts of the world, it is still illegal.

The doctor in St Vincent's Hospital had little choice and you might say he was doing us a favour. Peter had to leave their hospital and be readmitted to St Brendan's. I sat beside him in the ambulance to Grangegorman, both of us in a state of shock. Peter was quiet and subdued, still recovering from his experience of the night before. I knew he wouldn't want to go back there. I didn't want to lose him to that place either, but I had no choice.

We arrived. He looked back at me longingly as he was taken away. I picked up the pen on the desk in front of me and signed the form that committed Peter to stay as an involuntary patient.

openhearted

An old school friend reminded me recently how I once gave my dinner money to a girl in our class who was collecting for Guide Dogs for the Blind. I couldn't believe she had remembered that from our schooldays in the 1950s. I certainly don't. I wouldn't even class myself as a dog lover. Yet dogs seem to have been around me a lot, including a few that just followed us home to no. 8 Sandymount Green and stayed.

Apart from dogs, all sorts came through our door. Probably because the door was always on the latch. I left it that way, partly because one of my children always came home from school 'dying to go' and an open-door policy developed. Waifs and strays appeared, remained for a while and then left. There was an easygoing atmosphere and the children's school and college friends seemed to enjoy the lack of formality and the pizzas I made. I trusted my children and they were able to come and go as they pleased with the one exception – dinner was at six each evening and they had to be there for that.

After Peter died and the children were more independent, I became involved in community work, serving on committees for the local community week and arts festival. I was a member of the board of management of the primary school. I helped to start a youth club and became a leader. I helped with fundraising and sales of work. I enjoyed organizing, making things happen and being part of the community. A regular goody two shoes but I was pleasing myself as well. It was therapy and I enjoyed it.

Apart from 'good works', there was little I could do materially for anyone. My children were great at finding odd jobs and saved their money for trips away with the Guides or Scouts. I did not have any money to spare, but Travellers were always welcome at our door. At one stage the only difference in our circumstances was the tiled roof over my head and the fact that I wasn't discriminated against. Sister Agnes was the conveyor of clothes that my more affluent neighbours in Sandymount had discarded. I was always glad to receive what she brought, but we had an overflow. I saved what we didn't need for my Traveller friends, who were happy to receive them.

I like to think of myself as a socialist, but I was never actively involved in politics – although I did have a huge Vote for Labour poster in the front garden one election year. The socialist politician Richard Boyd Barrett must have noticed my left-wing tendencies. He came to the door one day suggesting I might like to join the Socialist Workers Party but that's as far as it went. I was very taken with the earnest young man and very nearly succumbed. To this day, some of my children tease me when he appears on television by saying, 'There's your boyfriend.'

Labour's Ruairi Quinn was Minister of Enterprise and Employment in 1994. He introduced the concept of Community Employment (CE), funded by the Department of Social Welfare. There was vast unemployment in the country at the time and this enterprise enables people who have been out of work for a while to re-engage in full-time employment and to be offered training. Ruairi lived close by and I was honoured to be asked to become a member of the Board of Sandymount Community Services, on which I still serve.

In 2002, I stepped down from the board for a few years to become the full-time supervisor. This job was the best paid work I ever had. It meant that I could put all the experience gained over the years to good use. There are many facets to being the supervisor of a CE programme. Accounts have to be kept scrupulously up to date, participants interviewed for jobs in the community and suitable training organized.

One young woman was a CE participant whose job it was to assist me in the office. As I got to know her, it became obvious that she was meant for bigger things than filling in forms. We had to do a lot of that. What she really wanted was to be a teacher. I managed, by bending the rules a little, to get her on the Leaving Certificate course at Ringsend Technical College. She went on to study at Maynooth University and, after much hard work, realized her ambition.

To be able to help people progress and improve their lives through the CE programme was a great source of joy and satisfaction for me. However, the most exciting part of my job was editing *NewsFour*, the local newspaper, published every two months. I had a team of six participants, with varying degrees of experience and literacy, and together we pulled it off. *NewsFour* went on to bigger things. It has its own website now.

It was while I was working for Sandymount Community Services that I fell down the stairs and broke my shoulder. It was a bad break and required an operation. As I lay in my bed, I could hear a young woman's voice coming from the neighbouring bed, speaking to the doctors. She told them exactly what they should be doing and how they should do it. In between coughs she reprimanded them about her medication.

When the curtains were pulled back I saw her. A young woman who looked extremely unwell. She introduced herself as Orla Tinsley and commiserated with me about the shoulder. She apologized for her coughing and said she hoped it wouldn't keep me awake.

I told her not to worry, I slept like a log.

It was Orla's first time in St Vincent's. Prior to that, when the cystic fibrosis got the better of her, she went to the Children's Hospital in Temple Street. Now she was eighteen. She had been living with CF all her life and knew what she was talking about.

'I shouldn't be here in this ward,' she said.

I looked around; there were six of us, mostly elderly women.

'I could get another infection,' she said.

In 2005, I knew little or nothing about the illness.

Listening to Orla, I wasn't sure if the doctors there were as well informed as she was.

Despite our age difference, we got on well. When Róisín called to visit me I introduced her to Orla. It would have happened anyway, but I like to think that introduction played a part in Orla's subsequent successful activism for people with CF. (Orla thought so too because she wrote about our meeting in her memoir, *Salty Baby*.)

Orla and I kept in touch. I was sitting at the coffee shop in St Vincent's Hospital, visiting her, in July 2011 when George and his two sisters passed by. I hadn't seen him for ages. George had worked with me in Sandymount Community Services some years back. He had been diagnosed with cancer of the liver earlier that year and had been receiving treatment at St Luke's. He was at St Vincent's that day to see a specialist about pain relief. I tried not to show my distress at seeing him, big George, looking so unlike himself. 'Good to see you, Ann,' he said. 'Any chance of getting that book done?'

I had promised I would help him with his book as a favour and my intentions were good but I had let it slide. It must have been a couple of years since I had worked on it. I had collected all George's pieces together and Eugene, a mutual friend, said he would help with the typesetting and inserting the pictures. But then my enthusiasm for the project faded. You know the way, you mean to do something and keep putting it into the drawer for another day. I saw George and Eugene from time to time and we promised to get together and finish it but we never did.

George was a recovering alcoholic. He could talk for hours about his addiction and how the good Lord had helped him to overcome it. He had been off the drink for sixteen years and had replaced it with AA meetings three times a week and a lot of eating. He was a ship's cook in his day. He had this habit of always telling you what he'd had for his dinner yesterday or what he was going to have tomorrow.

August and September would see George out blackberry picking. He was always very secretive about where he gathered the fruit. He made the most amazing blackberry and apple pies, on an industrial scale, and distributed them to his family and friends.

George loved ships. Although his seafaring days had been spent below deck in the galley, he was passionate about them. He was always talking about ships, it was his hobby, and he wanted to tell everyone of his experiences. He learned to use the computer but, when something went wrong and he needed help, he would call on me. 'I'll cook you a steak,' he'd say. That would do it for me and I would make time to help him and enjoy that overlarge steak surrounded by the best of vegetables. George ate like Desperate Dan.

The day after that meeting in St Vincent's, I went to see him in his house and gathered up the remaining photographs. Eugene and I worked on the book and took it to Snap Printing on Sir John Rogerson's Quay. By the time we had the first proof copy ready, George was in hospital. I sat beside him and we went through it, page by page. He was delighted and kept reminiscing as each page was turned. He dictated an introduction and we went to print.

When George left the hospital he was taken to Blackrock Hospice. His little book had to be launched and an old school friend of his, Charlie Murphy, who was Community Liaison Officer in the Dublin Port Company in Alexander Dock, helped with this. The launch took place in the boardroom on the top floor overlooking all the ships coming and going. On that particular day, the Cunard cruise ship *Queen Elizabeth* came into Dublin Bay.

The sun shone as George was wheeled in and all his friends and relatives were there to greet him. He signed copies of his book, which he had titled *Keep Her Head into the Wind: Irish Shipping Memories.* George laughed and chatted as everyone gathered around to congratulate him. When he left, we all knew we would never see him again and some people said it was like a living wake – a funny phrase that, but apt on this occasion. He died three days later on Monday 12 September 2011. It was an honour and privilege to be his friend. I will never forget George and those wonderful blackberry and apple pies.

*

Sometimes my enthusiasm for helping others has backfired on me. Sometimes I make decisions without thinking things through – with disastrous results.

After Peter died I received some unexpected funds from an insurance policy. I think his mother had taken a policy out many years before.

As always, when large sums of money come my way, I lost the head. A nice young man, who introduced himself as Alex, knocked on the door with a flyer in his hand telling me that they were doing a special offer on central heating. Radiators in every room and a new boiler for a very reasonable price was on offer. As I stood there in the hallway shivering, I jumped at it.

The next day Alex arrived with lots of pipes and paraphernalia and two other nice young men. By Friday my new central heating system was installed. Alex was in a terrible hurry to get off to another job and refused my offer of tea and cake to celebrate. I paid them in full and thought I was being very canny when I asked for a telephone number in case anything went wrong. 'No problem,' Alex said and handed me his card.

They could only have been round the corner in their HiAce van when the water started to pour out of the radiators. Brian managed to turn off the water supply while I ran to the telephone box to call them back.

I rang the number and the telephone was answered by a young woman.

'Cool Cut,' she said.

'Cool Cut?' I repeated.

'Yes, Cool Cut hairdressing salon,' she said, 'how can I help?'

When I asked for Alex, I was told there was no Alex there. Silly me.

There was still some money left from that windfall and a friend heard about it. The house she lived in with her husband and children was about to be taken from them because they had fallen behind with their rent. She asked me to lend her some money and promised to pay it back over the next year. I gave the money with a good heart, happy that I was in a position to help.

You can guess what happened. There were a few token payments of twenty pounds here and there, but gradually I began to realize it was unlikely I would see that money again.

When one of her children married, I was invited to attend the wedding, and I saw what seemed to me a very lavish affair for someone who supposedly had so little. It was making me unhappy and resentful so in the end I sent her a letter saying that I did not want any more repayments on the loan. She didn't reply.

That happened over thirty years ago and I like to think that I have become more circumspect and less impulsive in my old age, but it's difficult for old dogs to learn new tricks. My openheartedness has led me down dangerous paths sometimes and I fear it will continue until the day

I die. There are two definitions of openhearted. One is 'candidly straightforward', that's definitely me. The other is 'responsive to emotional appeal'. Yes, that's me too.

I was on one of my going-nowhere lockdown walks along the canal after we were finally let out. I was nearly at the bridge when I sat down to rest on the lock before continuing home. As I sat there with my headphones on, listening to my latest book, two women came along and they called to me. I took off the headphones.

'Any help?' one shouted. 'I'm desperate.'

She told me she was in a women's refuge and she needed money. She pulled down the neck of her jumper and showed me a bruise. 'I had to get away from him, he was going to kill me,' she said. Her friend nodded in agreement.

I sat there in the sunshine listening, not sure how to respond. The woman could see I was hesitating. 'I will get turned out tomorrow if I don't have the money to pay,' she called out. 'The children will have nowhere to sleep.'

I had a €50 note in my purse, and nothing much to spend it on, so I gave it to her. I didn't go over and hug her, but I stood up, went dangerously near, in social-distancing terms, and handed it to her. You can't throw a €50 note when you are standing beside a canal, anything could happen.

The women literally jumped up and down and hugged one another. I sat down again and watched as they walked away. It didn't matter what the woman did with the money; she needed it and I gave it. I know what it's like to be desperate.

I was in the supermarket recently and having difficulty at the do-it-yourself checkout. I was suitably masked and that blurs my glasses. In any case, I never seem to be able to identify the barcodes. One of the assistants saw me fumbling with the four packets of jam sugar for the marmalade I was making. This very pleasant young woman took over and in no time it was finished. I knew it was part of her job to get old ladies out of the way as quickly as possible but it didn't feel like that. I thanked her profusely and there were tears in my eyes as I turned to go.

That simple gesture got me thinking about the kindness people have shown me over the years.

Peter's taxi-driving career was fraught with problems. He was forever receiving fines for all sorts of misdemeanours that were unfathomable to me. He would take those annoying pieces of paper from the windscreen of his car, shove them into the glove compartment and forget them. But the gardaí didn't and it was the job of one of them to call at the house with a reminder to pay. The garda who called to our house came on his bike. He was a sympathetic man and almost apologized as he handed over copies of the outstanding fines. I took them from him but they remained unpaid.

Two gardaí in a car arrived at our door at six o'clock

one morning. They weren't as friendly as the one on the bike.

'I'm looking for Peter Ingle,' the first said.

'He's in bed,' I told them.

'Well, get him up,' the garda snapped.

Peter came downstairs and the two men bundled him into their car.

'Where are you taking him?' I asked.

'To Mountjoy, where do you think?' was the reply.

They took Peter away but, before they left, they handed me a sheaf of papers. When I added the jumble of figures, the fines came to over £200.

As I sat at the kitchen table gazing at the bills and wondering what I was going to do next, the friendly garda knocked on the door. He must have known that Peter was going to be arrested that morning. He explained that there was a loophole in the law and if I paid just one of those fines Peter would be released and the rest of them would be forgotten. This seemed unbelievable but the garda insisted it was true. The only difficulty now was that I didn't have £10, the price of the smallest one.

I went to the local hardware shop, where the chemist is now, on Sandymount Green. I told Miss Milligan and her assistant, Sarah, what had happened and asked for the loan of £10. This was quite a sum then, probably as much as a day's takings. I had no shame. I promised that they would have it back in a few days, when the Children's Allowance was due.

Ten pounds in hand, I went with that kind garda in his car to Mountjoy that afternoon. He parked around the corner in case any of his colleagues saw him. I knocked nervously on the tall wooden door of the prison, still not really believing that I would bring Peter home. But it worked. Paying just one of those fines meant Peter was released. The law is an ass, they say, but no matter, it worked in our favour.

I never saw that garda again, but I hope he found a job more suited to his personality. I paid Miss Milligan back as promised.

Asking for help is not always easy nor well-received. It has been my misfortune to have been obliged to look for assistance from Community Welfare Officers over the years. Some of them were obviously unhappy in their work and barely acknowledged my presence in the room as they fidgeted with the forms. But not all of them. On one occasion I met a very kind and sympathetic officer who made a lasting impact on our lives.

Peter had been in St Brendan's for five weeks and was due for discharge. I was applying for a disability allowance and bus pass for him. The relieving officer quickly sorted out the paperwork and then he sat back in his chair and asked me how I was. This was the first time anyone in that social welfare office had asked that question.

I went for it. I didn't say I was grand, coping, I told

the truth. I told him that when Peter came home life would be hard for all of us. I told him that Peter's injections made him weak and unhappy. He was miserable, I was miserable. Peter said his life was just not worth living. 'It's no wonder,' I said, 'that he wants to kill himself, I would too.'

I said all this without expecting any help. I just needed someone to listen but this man did more than that. He told me of a doctor friend of his, Mark Hartman, who might be able to help, and he gave me his number.

I telephoned Dr Hartman, made an appointment and got up on my bike and went to Eaton Square. It was a large, imposing house in that beautiful square in Monkstown and I was a little intimidated as I rang the bell. I needn't have worried. Mark Hartman said that my reservations about Peter's injections were valid. He recommended that his medication should be changed to tablets and said he would inform the doctor in charge of Peter's treatment. I realized then that this man must have some sort of special authority.

Mark Hartman was one of the most eminent practitioners in his field. He died in 1994 and in his obituary I read: 'We tend to be rather insular in Ireland but Mark gave to us something of the universal. He was an intellectual in the true European sense.' For me, Mark Hartman was a compassionate, down-to-earth doctor who listened.

I never saw that young man from the social welfare

office again. I don't even know his name. But without him I would not have met Dr Hartman and Peter would not have had the benefit of his care and attention. It changed the last years of Peter's life, and mine too.

The kindness of those two men gave Peter relief from the effects of being over-medicated. It gave me a semblance of my husband back. Although he would never be that beautiful boy I had met in Newquay, we could talk again. He was able to show his love for me and the children, something that hadn't happened for a long time.

I appreciate and treasure all the well-meant acts of charity from good people that have come my way, I really do. But it's not always easy. After I had been widowed for some time, one of my son's college friends, who was a frequent visitor, told his mother about our circumstances. She organized a coffee morning. I was in the habit of fundraising for all sorts – the local Multiple Sclerosis Society of Ireland situated a few doors away from me, the Girl Guides, the Scouts – I was always ready to help. The idea of me being the recipient of the largesse of ladies in Dalkey did not come easily to me. But I smiled as the young man proudly handed over the money. And I sent a letter of thanks to his mother expressing my gratitude.

Sometimes I didn't accept what was offered. One day a Sandymount lady came to my door and asked if I would like a job ironing for her household. I barely ironed anything in my own home, unlike some I knew who ironed their tea towels. I am sure she was trying to be kind, but I politely declined her offer.

On another occasion I did not even attempt to hide my disdain. The parish priest in affluent Sandymount was having difficulty finding enough local candidates for the annual Christmas dinner for the homeless provided by the Knights of Saint Columbanus. He came to my door offering my family the opportunity to attend. I found this hurtful and I do not think it was pride on my part. Well, maybe just a little. I would make a Christmas for my children without leaving the house and subjecting them to dinner with strangers. I declined his insensitive offer.

Sometimes, however, you take an unexpected offer of help without a moment's hesitation. Two days after Peter died I suddenly got the idea that his body could be used to help someone. I was in the middle of cooking chips, but I could not wait to tell the hospital. I rushed next door to use the telephone. It took me a while to contact the right person, and I was happy when they said it wasn't too late for his eyes to be donated. By the time I was back in the kitchen, the chip pan was on fire. I smothered the flames, threw the pan out of the back door and looked around me. The yellow walls, which I had painted so lovingly to bring the sunshine into the house, were black. Out of nowhere, men appeared with buckets and scrubbing brushes. They came, they went, in a haze of smoke. I couldn't identify any of them.

During the days after Peter died, we were inundated

with casseroles and cakes. Sometimes people just left things on the doorstep.

I wanted a memorial card for Peter printed with the words of one of his favourite Percy French songs, 'In the Woods of Gortnamona'. The printer refused payment.

The kindness shown to us by neighbours, friends and some people I didn't even know was overwhelming and quite wonderful. No words.

At Christmas, the hampers from St Vincent de Paul were gratefully and joyfully received. The people on those committees all over Ireland do great work but it's the generosity of the people who donate that make it possible. The money Sister Agnes pulled out of that magical black bag of hers came from a collection in the church. Every year in the Star of the Sea there was a special collection for Sister Agnes and her work. Each one of those people who contributed helped me and others in the parish.

Anyone and everyone who ever helped my children, helped me too. There was always work to be had for the family in the local shops. Scout and Guide leaders giving of their time to my children were crucial for their growth and well-being. It's a bit late now, but thank you.

There were so many different ways people showed their kindness. But there is one particular act that was unique and utterly unforgettable. We lived three doors down from the local chipper. Mama and Papa Borza must have thought up this great idea: each Christmas Eve, their son, Bruno, would appear at the door with what was left in the cooker. Steaming brown paper bags full of chips, smoked cod, onion rings, sausages-in-batter, spice burgers, the lot. I can smell it now. The delight and excitement of free food from Borza's started the Christmas festivities like nothing else.

All those wonderful people in my life have helped me in different ways and I hope they know how much it means to me. There is an art to receiving graciously. I hope I managed it.

Now I am old, I find myself prefacing requests for help with phrases such as 'If you can spare the time' and 'It's not that important but . . .'. I try not to bother my family with my old-lady problems. They are all very busy people. I know they don't like that – they would do anything for me – but I just don't want to be a bother. A lot of my friends are like that too. But, really, I know I should snap out of it.

Today, in my old age, I resolve to take anything that is offered with dignity and suppress any pride that might still be lurking.

ward 23

If I had known what was going to happen to Peter at St Brendan's during his third stay there I would have taken him with me and torn up the involuntary detention form I had signed. The look on his face as we said good-bye haunted me. After I left he was put into Ward 23, reserved for 'special cases'. This was a place for people who were considered a danger to themselves or so far down the road of insanity as to never return.

I was not prepared for what I saw on the first evening when I went in to see him. I had visited Peter in St Brendan's before and the conditions were never ideal, but what I encountered now shocked and horrified me.

To gain access to see him, I had to go through several big, heavy doors. It was the clanging of the large bunch of keys the male nurse used to lock each door behind us that I remember most vividly. The further we went, the more it came to look like a Gothic mansion in a horror film.

The visiting area was open to all the patients. Peter and I were never alone. People walked around aimlessly, some chanting, some in a state of undress, some just standing leaning against the wall. The walls were stone blocks, like the inside of a church or monastery, cold and damp to the touch. It felt to me as if we had been transported to a different century. This was a lunatic asylum. I couldn't wait to get out of there that first evening. But I went again the next night. I went every night. I had to.

Many of the patients did not receive visitors. When they saw me sitting with Peter they came over and joined us, desperate for someone different to see and talk to. They never made much sense, but it was a distraction. Peter didn't have a lot to say and he didn't seem to mind his fellow inmates muscling in. I just went along with it and tried my best to make conversation, sensible or otherwise.

I was intrigued by one man who looked sane enough. He was to be seen sitting at a little table writing. One day, as I was leaving, he pushed a letter into my hand. 'Please give this to the appropriate authorities,' he said. He had a very cultured voice and was most polite. He might once have been a priest. I took the letter from him.

Dear Reverend Father

On behalf of myself and other 'patients' in Unit 23 of this infamous institution, I would like to impress upon you that there are many men here, of all races, creeds and walks of life, virtually all Irish Catholics like myself. It so happens that, after starting this letter, a patient came to our table asking why having made his first confession in years, he was not able to receive communion in or out of the wards.

I hope you will have the courage our faith demands and <u>see to it</u> that this outrageous situation is rectified forthwith.

Yours in Maria (Legionary of Mary)

He asked me to deliver it. I never did. I couldn't see the point. Nobody was going to take any notice of an inmate from Ward 23.

Having committed Peter to this horrible place weighed heavily on my conscience. But really I had no choice. And very slowly Peter did improve. I was so grateful to hear him talking coherently again. But it must have been terrifying coming to your senses and finding yourself in those conditions.

The routine was rigid and the only relief was going to the occupational therapy block where menial tasks were undertaken, supposedly as a means of rehabilitation. Back on Ward 23, he was a prisoner, locked up and surrounded by men who were deranged and unable to communicate in any rational way. Peter was miserable and longing to get home.

His delusions seemed to have faded and he stopped talking of suicide. I asked if he could come home for the weekend and permission was granted. We were both happy and relieved. It also meant that this was a step towards him being allowed to come home permanently.

That weekend was very special and I tried to make everything as normal as possible. I had painted the sitting room while he was away and my colour choice was an indication of the state of my own mind and emotions. Two walls were a violent pink and the others a darker tone; looking back, they were not conducive to a peaceful ambience. I needn't have worried about my inappropriate choice of colours because Peter hardly noticed and certainly didn't care, he was just happy to be home.

I had started to paint the wooden kitchen chairs a variety of colours, more as occupational therapy for me in those strange times. He helped for a bit but, really, all he wanted to do was sit in the armchair, talk to the children and watch the television. Having been so long away from people and real life, it was a novelty for him just being there with us. I decided we would go to the pictures on Saturday evening.

The film I chose was *One Flew over the Cuckoo's Nest* – a story about an American psychiatric hospital. I hadn't done my research and as the film progressed and Jack Nicholson was led into the psychiatric ward, I realized my mistake. However horrible their circumstances with the dreaded Nurse Ratched in charge, the Oregon State Hospital, where the filming took place, was luxurious compared to what Peter had experienced. And here on the screen, the inmates were engaged in group therapy, something that did not happen in Ward 23.

I looked at Peter as the film unfolded and saw him smiling as Nicholson addressed his fellow patients: 'What do you think, you're crazy or something?'

At the Academy Awards, the film won five Oscars, so

perhaps my choice wasn't so bad. Don't mind me, I am just trying to justify bringing the poor man to see that film on his weekend release from a lunatic asylum.

I escorted him back to Brendan's on Sunday night. I don't know why but I had convinced myself that he wouldn't be put back into Ward 23. I was wrong. When I visited on Monday, I found him there once again and I was furious. I told the nurse that this was unacceptable and asked for him to be removed to another ward immediately. 'I have no authority to do a thing like that,' he said.

I was determined to do something to get Peter out of there and when I got home I wrote a letter to the doctor in charge. I wasn't going to post it as that would take too long and I wanted immediate action. I knew I wouldn't be able to take it to the hospital myself as I had to mind Michael and the other children I was looking after so I kept Eddie off school and sent him to deliver the letter to the psychiatrist in charge of Peter's welfare.

I can see Eddie now, setting out on his bike early that morning, with me hoping he would find his way to Grangegorman. I needn't have worried. He delivered the letter into Dr Burke's hands as he had been asked to do. This was a great achievement for a twelve-year-old. I was so grateful and relieved when he came home with the news that the mission was accomplished and sent him off to school.

Dear Dr Burke

I wanted to call in to see you this morning but due to domestic circumstances this proved impossible. I have, however, sent my son to deliver this by hand.

Peter was home for the weekend and the few days passed very happily for us all. We did some work in the house. You can imagine how much of a wrench it was for Peter to return to 23. It would seem to me as a layman that the more adjusted to the outside world and the realities of life one becomes, the less attractive grows Unit 23.

I visited him last night and the locked door seemed ludicrous after the freedom he had enjoyed 24 hours previously. He said how much he would like to be home permanently – he mentioned that you said it would be a while yet and asked me my estimation of a 'while'. Dr McCarthy already said that she could not estimate how long he would be required to be with you. I appreciate this and am very pleased with Peter's progress. With all due respect, however, I feel that Peter in his present condition is not now in the best of places for progress to be made. He needs more interaction with his fellow man and unfortunately his fellow patients where he is now are not up to it.

Would a transfer to Unit 3 be possible? Alternatively, I did mention to Dr McCarthy that the premises you have in Clonskeagh would be nearer here but I believe there were redecorations taking place there at the time I asked about it. Maybe when they are finished you might think it suitable for him to be there.

The other alternative, of course, is his discharge. Dr
McCarthy said she would try to get a bus pass for him so that
he could continue in the workshop when he came home. She feels
the work habit should be kept up and of course I agree but only
wish the work was a little more varied as when I ask Peter what
he was doing to-day in the therapy unit he replies 'sanding down'.
I have done that myself when the odd chair needed repainting
and found it tedious and boring. However, I am not a patient
and should not judge my reactions in the same light I suppose.

I shall be most grateful if you will do something for him as
I feel a move at this time would boost his morale and reaffirm
that he is improving. Perhaps you will talk to Peter about it.

Yours sincerely
Ann Ingle

Reading this letter now, I have to smile; I can imagine
the doctor smiling too. *Who is this woman attempting to tell*
me what to do with my patients? But when I went to see Peter
that evening he was in Unit 3. He told me that he had
been put there that afternoon unexpectedly and couldn't
understand how it had happened. I felt a great sense of
victory that my letter had had the required effect. It made
a big difference to Peter being situated in these new sur-
roundings. He was happier and so was I.

Now that he was in Unit 3 and away from all those
locked doors and clanking keys, I decided that when
Rachael and Brian made their confirmation I would bring

them in to see him. Arrangements were made for us to visit Peter in a conservatory at the side of the ward, which gave us privacy. Peter was happy and proud to see them. He didn't say a lot but just kept smiling.

Rachael and Brian were not quite sure what they were doing there but gave their father hugs and showed off their new clothes. They behaved as if it was the most ordinary thing in the world to visit a mental institution on your confirmation day. On the way home, we got off the bus in O'Connell Street and went to Flanagans restaurant for a special treat.

Life went on at home as usual. I visited every evening and Peter continued to improve. The day was soon approaching when he would be home with me again. I wanted that more than anything and so did he.

At last Peter was released from St Brendan's and a new phase of our life began. His medication was changed and things improved for all of us. I wanted Peter to stay with me forever and never have to go back into that place again.

sing out, sisters

When you are young, people often ask, 'What do you want to be when you grow up?' I asked two of my grand-children that very question yesterday, and one said she wanted to own a drama school, the other said she wanted to be a baker. When asked that question as a child I would reply with great confidence 'an actress or a singer'. My father often took me to the Hackney Empire, a music hall in London, and that's where I got the notion – I watched those glamorous young women on the stage and dreamed of being up there with them. On holiday in Cornwall, I went out on the boat every morning mack-erel fishing with the same boatman. We would sail off and begin to sing – well, I would sing, and he joined in with such ditties as 'On a Slow Boat to China' or 'Charmaine'. I sang out loud and clear.

My illusions were shattered on the day we went to Southend. On the pier there was a Voice-O-Graph machine. It looked like a telephone box. My father put some money into the slot and I sang for three minutes, at the end of which time a six-inch vinyl record popped out like a bar of chocolate from a vending machine. I couldn't wait to get home to hear my rendition of 'You Call Everybody Darling'.

I put my tiny vinyl on to my record player and couldn't believe my ears. I was astounded. I didn't sound like one of the Andrews Sisters, more like Donald Duck's girlfriend, Daisy. As I listened to myself singing I thought of that boatman and what he had endured. I was devastated, my anticipated career was over before it began and after that I barely hummed for years.

But I can't help it, now I burst into song and am so grateful to my grandchildren who don't seem to realize that I sing 'Christopher Robin' and 'The Wheels on the Bus' off-key. Well, maybe they do but it doesn't seem to matter. A few Christmases ago, I was taken by Lily Allen's song 'Somewhere Only We Know' and wanted desperately to sing it. A singing teacher, who happened to be a friend of my daughter, coached me. The result was acceptable, and I boldly sang for my family that Christmas. I do hope someone recorded it on their mobile phone.

That was a one-off. At family gatherings it's difficult to get a word in edgeways, never mind a tune. I mostly sit back and listen. 'Don't talk over me,' I say, 'Don't interrupt,' but they don't always hear. The thing is, sometimes if they stop me in mid flow, I am liable to forget what I am about to say. It might be gone forever or at least until I'm lying in bed the next morning.

In many ways we elderly people are at the height of our powers as regards wisdom and life experience but people don't have time to take notice. Appearance is everything and the words that come out of a grey-haired old lady with a bit of a limp don't seem to have much impact most of the time. Jane Fonda can get away with it, but then she's Jane Fonda. I do not aspire to be like that wonderful woman, not possible, but I want to make my point. I need my voice to be heard amongst all the clamour for attention.

Of course, the best and easiest way to ensure the audience is listening is to meet with people your own age. We know to speak a little slower and a little louder when we are conversing. In normal times, every Friday morning I go to St Andrew's Resource Centre in Pearse Street to join my writing companions. We call ourselves the PS Writers Group. I joined them in 2014, but they have been going for twenty years or more. There are ten in the group and only three are under eighty. A mature gathering.

Every week someone suggests a topic and we go home and write a story. We meet at 10.30 and start by having a cup of tea or coffee before we each read out our work. Strictly speaking, they are not stories, more like flash fiction because they usually run to about 1,000 words. We only have the room for ninety minutes so we have to be quick.

Inevitably, we discuss current affairs, and sometimes there are differences of opinion. Usually they are about the media, racism and sometimes sexuality in one form or another. In 2013, the debate on repealing the Eighth Amendment to the Irish Constitution began, so whether Ireland's ban on abortion should be retained became yet another topic to add to our sorting-out-the-world conversations.

Mary Fleming, who has been a guiding light in the PS Writers from the beginning, has become a friend. She is a broad-minded woman with a great sense of humour and a family who are prominent in the arts and music. We are alike, I like to think, in many ways, except one. Mary is a devout Catholic. She sings in the choir at her local church. So when it came to abortion and the Repeal the Eighth Campaign, we differed.

The production team of the *Irish Times Women's Podcast* was looking for older people to go on air and talk about their views on abortion. I jumped at the chance and, when they asked me if I knew someone who held the opposite opinion to mine, I thought of Mary. We sat facing one another in the studio. I told her I'd had an illegal abortion when I was twenty-one under traumatic circumstances and she sympathized. The conversation went back and forth but neither of us gave any ground. She believed that abortion was wrong and I believed that every woman should have the right to choose. I do not know if it had any effect on listeners. We were just two elderly women with differing points of view. I like to think we had a balanced discussion.

We left the *Irish Times* office as we came in, good friends. And I had made a discovery. It is possible to have respect and love for someone who has diametrically opposing views to yourself. I was never really sure of that before.

The Repeal campaign was a challenge to me personally because of Róisín. She looked to me for direction as she was considering telling the story of her own abortion in her book of columns entitled *Public Displays of Emotion.* I was worried that she would lose readers and that her career would be damaged, and I told her so. She agonized over it, we both did. She asked the advice of good friends and, finally, she made the right decision.

In September 2015, after the piece about her abortion appeared in the *Irish Times*, Róisín was interviewed by the late broadcaster Marian Finucane. I sat there with her in the RTÉ studio. I was very nervous. Now it wasn't just the readers of the *Irish Times* who would know but listeners all over Ireland.

The actor and writer Tara Flynn joined us afterwards and as we sat outside a pub in Donnybrook drinking our coffees. Tara had also talked publicly about having had an abortion. I listened to the two of them, overawed by their commitment and passion for the cause. There was no stopping all those brave women in Ireland who were campaigning at the time. They were determined to change the legislation that was sending thousands of Irish women to England and further afield for a procedure that should have been available to them in Ireland.

Later in the campaign, I saw Tara Flynn perform her one-woman show *Not a Funny Word* in the Project Theatre. With song and dance she told the story of her experience of travelling to Holland for an abortion. I wished my friend Mary could have seen it. No words of mine would ever be as powerful as that performance.

In April 2017, there was a fundraising event taking place in the Olympia Theatre and Róisín wanted us both to go on stage and discuss our abortions. I was reluctant for a number of reasons. For a start, standing in front of 2,000 people on the stage of a theatre was not something you did every day, although the idea wasn't completely alien to me. At the time, the acting bug had got me. I had been rehearsing for some months with Oonagh Murphy and Noelle Browne on a play Noelle had written for Bealtaine called *Creaking*. I loved it, and it left me a little stage-struck. The whole family came to see my performance and I think that was how Róisín got the idea.

Another reason was I couldn't quite grasp the relevance of my experience compared to Róisín's. They had taken place forty years apart. But then I realized that they were connected simply because when I got pregnant in 1960 abortion was illegal in the UK, just like it still was in Ireland. It wasn't until the Abortion Act of 1967 was passed that women could legally and safely have their pregnancies terminated. Prior to this, women from wealthy families could afford to go to private consultants in London's Harley Street and other cities. But thousands of women resorted to back-street abortions, which in some cases resulted in permanently damaging their health or even death. Why did everyone think being unmarried and pregnant was such a catastrophe that death was preferable?

Apart from thinking my experience might not resonate with younger people, I knew that everyone in that audience would be pro-choice already so it wouldn't change anyone's mind. And when I heard that Panti Bliss, Neil Hannon and Mary Black were performing that night, I was overwhelmed at the idea of being on the same stage as luminaries such as them. I had my excuses but Róisín kept on at me. I talked with other members of the family. Some encouraged me, others were not so sure. It wasn't until the last minute that I made my decision. I had been given this opportunity to stand up and speak out and I wasn't about to let it go.

Rachael, Michael and my granddaughter Hannah were in the audience that night as Róisín and I sat on the stage and talked. I told the story of my abortion. At the end of our discussion Róisín asked my opinion on how the campaign could be won and I replied: 'By being gentle and understanding and kind and acknowledging that for every single woman and every single crisis pregnancy there is a different story. We have to do this with love. If people look at one another with love and empathy then maybe we can win.'

Then she asked, 'And what will you do when an anti-choice person comes knocking on your door?'

And I said: 'I will ask them in for a cup of tea, I will tell them that they are perfectly entitled to their views. I'll tell them if I had my way nobody would have to have an abortion but that isn't realistic and the alternative is people suffer. Nobody *wants* to have an abortion. I'd ask them to leave our daughters and our granddaughters and all the men and families involved to make their own very difficult decisions that will affect the rest of their lives.'

When I left the stage I knew I had done the right thing. As an older woman, I had been listened to and the audience clapped and roared their approval. A young man came up to me as I left the Olympia that night and shook my hand. 'You spoke so well,' he said, 'congratulations.'

Congratulations! The experience and opinions of this old lady meant as much as anyone else's.

I continued in my own small way to campaign, gaining more confidence every day. It helped that Deirdre Duffy was my next-door neighbour at the time and she kept me up to speed. Deirdre is a barrister and she became campaign manager along with former Labour Party official Amy Rose Harte. My friend Aoife McArdle ferried me to various events where I learned more about the campaign and how to go about getting that all-important Yes vote. 'Together for Yes' brought a number of different organizations together, which made our voices stronger.

Every time I got into a taxi I engaged the driver in talk about the campaign. I didn't hold back and spoke out with assurance. I was gratified to find that most of those drivers were supporters. I talked about it at every opportunity because every vote counted.

On 25 May 2018, 1,439,981 people in Ireland said Yes to allow women to make their own decision to access abortion in their own country.

I joined the celebrations in Dublin Castle with my granddaughters Joya and Priya. Fianna Fáil leader Micheál Martin was there as a bystander, just like me. He was leaning over the railings and he smiled as I put out my hand to shake his. He had supported the campaign in spite of the views of his party and I wanted to say thank you to him for his courage. But I didn't, I just shook his hand and I think he knew.

All the hard work paid off and now on the island of Ireland women have access to abortion facilities. It is not the case worldwide. Some women in 2021 are still risking their lives as I did in 1961 when I had an illegal abortion.

So many women, young and old, spoke out for change and I was one of them. I am happy that I took the challenge.

Many women before me have been courageous throughout their lives. I watched a programme called *Mad, Bad and Dangerous: A Celebration of Difficult Women*, a documentary series of interviews, in the Dublin Fringe Festival last year. Six well-known Irish women over seventy years of age interviewed each other. I listened to Lelia Doolan, Margaretta D'Arcy, Bernadette McAliskey, Paula Cummins, Jo Murphy-Lawless and Nell McCafferty talking about their lives and opinions, and I saluted them from afar. Emma O'Grady, who created and directed the event, said in an interview, 'Over time, with older women, it's as if their volume gets turned down; we just don't listen to them any more.'

Older women have spent too long not being listened to. We don't have a sell-by date, our voices have not expired, and we deserve to be heard.

Just don't ask me to sing.

things change

That 'for better or for worse' vow you sign up to when you get married is a tricky one. I would recommend you think long and hard before you put your signature to it. Maybe it would be for the best to leave it out altogether. Things change all the time, people change.

The man I married was not the man I ended up with. I was married for twenty years to one man. But that man changed. First, he was just my beautiful nature boy, a fun-loving lover, who sang like a bird. He had secrets which he kept from me until after we were married. We got over that together and moved on.

Peter could never quite get things right and my function in the marriage was one of picking up the pieces, sorting it all out and making things better. Peter resented the authority of the 'boss', but even when he worked for himself as a taxi driver, things didn't improve. But all through this, he loved me. We loved one another. Peter charmed his way through it all and we survived.

There came a time when that loving stopped and for me that was unbearable. I ran away, taking the children with me. It was, I thought, a final forever thing. Peter wouldn't let me go and I returned home to start another chapter of our lives together.

Life with Peter was always a struggle but I became accustomed to it. I wasn't prepared and could never have imagined that Peter would lose touch with reality the way he did. After the delusions began and he was diagnosed with schizophrenia, a different life began for the two of us. I became his minder. I had another child to look after.

Peter was in and out of hospital for five years before he eventually took his own life. It sounds crazy but the last year of his life was a relief, for me and the children anyway.

There was no expectation that Peter would ever work again. He had a disability pension and a bus pass. He no longer talked of religion. His medication had been changed and now he could sit without shaking. He had the energy to walk for more than a few steps. I knew where he was, what he was doing and where he was going every day. And there was a calm.

Peter took Michael to school for me in the mornings.[1] They walked together, usually going the long way round, but unfortunately sometimes they came home again. Michael was a reluctant school-goer and Peter did not have the heart to insist.

We did all sorts of things that would have been impossible in the preceding years. My diary for 1979 reminds me of an Awareness project running that year organized by Dublin Corporation. During the school holidays there were free exhibitions and a programme of visits

---

1. Even as I write I can hear my daughters getting cross with 'for me' – that's the 'internalized patriarchy' raising its ugly head again, they'll say.

to art galleries and museums. Peter came along with me and the youngest children, walking with his new slow and deliberate gait, but he was there. He even came to the zoo with me and the children I was still looking after. He became another pair of hands and I couldn't have managed that trip without him. He was exhausted by the time we came home but he made it.

So many happy times. Peter went to Coliemore Harbour fishing with Eddie, Brian, little Peter and Michael, something that would have been impossible just six months before. We took the bus out to Dún Laoghaire and had a picnic on the pier. Peter and I attended the wedding of his niece, all dressed up like any other married couple. We even went to the theatre, sitting in a box that John Molloy had organized for us. All this sounds ordinary, just the everyday things that families do, but for me they were unexpected and wonderful. It had been a long time since Peter had been able to be properly part of the family.

One day he took the children for a walk along the old railway tracks in Sandymount and he came home with a plant in his hand with bright green and shiny leaves. Beneath the leaves was a long white root, like a parsnip. 'It's horseradish,' he said, 'you can make sauce out of it.'

This was a little miracle for me. Peter had noticed and identified something I would never have known about or even noticed. The only horseradish sauce I had ever seen before came from a jar. My eyes streamed as I hacked away at that bulb and Peter laughed.

'I knew that would happen,' he said.

I mixed the grated horseradish with some cream and mayonnaise and found a jar to put it in. We had it with rib steak that night. This is a very vivid memory. It meant so much more than just a jar of very hot sauce that could blow your head off. It was a little thing but it gave me hope.

He was able to go to the pub now and again too. He would sit quietly nursing his pint, not the life and soul like before. But, still, he went and I was happy for him. You could almost believe he was happy too, after a pint or two.

Peter could make love to me on occasion, if I pestered him. That was important to me. When I closed my eyes, he was still the man I had fallen in love with all those years ago.

Peter's obsessions appeared to have gone but now and again that faraway look came over him. I was always on my guard. I continued to go to meetings of the Schizophrenic Society in the hope that I might hear of some miraculous medical breakthrough. Silly me.

In my diary I read an entry that says, 'I will go mad if I don't have a kindred spirit to talk with.' I could talk to Peter but it was a little like talking to a child. Nothing heavy, no politics, no opinions sought or given. Peter was there in body, but intellectually I was on my own. I never knew what was going on in his head. When I did venture to ask his opinion on important matters, he replied, 'You know what is best,' and that was that.

Peter was excited when Sister Agnes suggested a trip to Lourdes for the two of us. I was wary at first, worried that it might send Peter down the rabbit hole of religion again. I took a chance. Agnes got us a place on the Dublin Diocesan Pilgrimage to Lourdes which took place, and still does, every September.

Lourdes is a small town in the foothills of the Pyrenees. It wasn't of any interest to anybody until 1858 when the Virgin Mary said to Bernadette Soubirous, a young peasant girl, 'Go drink at the spring and wash yourself there.' Catholics have been visiting ever since in the hope of a cure.

I had no expectation that the Lord might intervene in Peter's illness, but it was a diversion. It was a wonderful few days, and Peter and I immersed ourselves in the atmosphere and the baths. The water was freezing and I was amazed to find I was almost dry when I came out of the water, barely needing a towel. But it was not a miracle, just the hot weather that dried me so quickly. The highlight for Peter was the large pitcher of lager he had on the night before we left. There was no harm. Peter's problem was not alcohol and if it made him happy that was all that mattered.

I had similar misgivings about the Pope's visit to

Ireland. Peter was really anxious to see him. It was Katie's first birthday, 29 September 1979. I stayed at home with her while Peter set off to the Phoenix Park with young Peter and Michael. The other children had gone too, with the Scouts or with their friends. It was a novelty just being at home alone with Katie, but I worried that seeing the Pope might trigger something in Peter's mind. I waited anxiously until they came home, but I needn't have worried. They had called into the pub on their way back. Michael was high on crisps and his father a little the worse for wear. Young Peter was just tired after the long walk.

When Christmas came around that year, Peter looked at the tree, the big window with the glittering mural the children had painted, and all the decorations, and said, 'Do you do this every year?' I suppose he is not the only man in the world who takes for granted all the work that women put in to creating a happy Christmas but at least Peter had an excuse.

It was as if he had been living in a dream and now had suddenly woken up. I believe he realized in that moment all that I had done for him and the family during our life together. He put his arms around me and hugged me so tight that I thought I would break. It was a gesture that stayed with me and something that I cherish, even today as I write these words.

Peter's condition improved so much with the new medication. I was happy for him and stronger in myself.

Our lives had changed for the better. I wasn't kidding myself, I knew that Peter would never be the same again. The tablets were part of the reason for that but if he didn't take them then the delusions would start again and where would we be.

What I didn't realize was that if Peter could discover horseradish and live a relatively normal life, he could also work out for himself how he wanted to die.

When he came home one evening without his favourite jumper, and told me he had given it to a nice woman in the pub who had admired it, maybe I should have known. But I didn't, I just kissed him and went upstairs to bed.

i like peter

Peter took his life on 25 September 1980. It was just another ordinary Thursday. I woke early and stretched out my arm for Peter, the way I always did. He wasn't there. Róisín's eight-year-old head lay on the pillow. She was always at that, bed-hopping. She looked so angelic when she was asleep.

I can't say I knew straight away. But seeing her in the bed where he should have been frightened me. I had left Peter sitting at the kitchen table the night before. He had said he would be up later, so where was he?

I ran downstairs. He had to be asleep on the sofa in the front room. But he wasn't. I went into the kitchen and all I could see was a scattering of coins on the table.

I saw the back door was open. He must have got up early and gone outside. That was it.

I went out into the garden and there he was.

He wasn't hanging from the apple tree. Not like in cowboy films when they string someone up. Peter was sitting on our stepladder with a blue rope around his neck. He had sat there and simply fallen backwards until the rope tightened and he was gone.

I looked up into the tree. I knew there was nothing I could do for him. Not any more.

I ran to my neighbour's to call the gardaí. Back in the house, I could hear the children stirring upstairs.

'Don't look out of the window,' I shouted over and over again. 'Don't look out of the window.'

The gardaí came with an ambulance and took Peter

away. They left that thick blue rope on top of the washing machine. I sat cuddling Katie. It felt like there was a hole in my chest. That must be what people call a broken heart.

On the last evening of Peter's life, he went to the pub for a pint. He came home without his jumper. 'I gave it away,' he said. 'There was a woman in the pub, she said she liked it, so I gave it to her.'

He loved that jumper. That should have been a clue but I missed it.

That night, Peter sat at the table and wrote his last words; not a will and testament, just his last words. He wrote them on the nearest thing he could find, a Ladybird book. He opened it at the page where it said, 'I like Peter,' and wrote:

I loved you the best Ann. I can't stick it anymore. Forgive me. God bless you and all the children. Peter

He emptied his pockets and scattered the loose change on the table. He went into the garden with that thick blue rope, placed the stepladder beside the tree, put the rope around the tree and then around his neck, sat on the top step of the ladder and let himself fall backwards.

Peter had thought it through. He couldn't risk the branches of that old apple tree letting him down. This time he wasn't going to make a mistake. One day, years later, that old apple tree just fell over.

Peter had asked for my forgiveness. In my eyes, what he did was a supreme act of courage and love for me and the children.

Forgive him? There was nothing to forgive.

The jumper lady came to the door a few weeks after Peter's death. She wanted me to have it. My first instinct was to take it from her. And I did. I hugged it to me. It was damp with my tears when I handed it back. We were both crying.

'He wanted you to have it,' I said. 'He told me.'

Imagine, the last conversation I had with Peter was about a jumper. If only I had known I would have told him again how much I loved him. *Always have, always will,* I'd say.

I would have talked about the children. How Michael loves to walk to school with him because he always goes the long way round. How Peter says I am rubbish at arithmetic and wants Daddy to help. How Róisín loves to sing with him because she says I sound like a cuckoo. Even the baby Katie knew that. She always falls asleep in his arms when he croons 'Too-Ra-Loo-Ra-Loo-Ral', just like Bing Crosby.

I would have reminded him that Brian is going to be famous one day, a star. That Eddie wants to become a doctor and find a cure for what ails him. How Sarah is starting college and how delighted he will be at her graduation. How he is so proud of Rachael, the sanest person in Ireland, he calls her.

I would have said that one day we would have grand-children and they would love him. I would have talked about the Strand and the mountains that he loved so much. I would have promised holidays in the country. Anything, everything.

And if he really had to go, I wish I could have been with him, just to say goodbye.

before i go

I did it. I succeeded. I finished. Maybe when the first copy rolls off the printing press I will get that tattoo I promised myself: *I wrote a memoir*. I will ask the woman to ink it in blue – that's my favourite colour.

I haven't tripped over once since I started writing and I am determined not to have any more falls. No one will ever have to pick me up again. My voice is being heard and if anyone buys this book then I will no longer be invisible.

Maybe I will be interviewed and someone will ask me about Peter and how much he meant to me. He has been gone for a long time now, but it's important everyone should know that, despite all my shenanigans, I loved him the best, just as he did me.

On the first anniversary of Peter's death in September 1981, I had a memorial for him published in the news-paper, with the poem 'Remember', by Christina Rossetti.

> Remember me when I am gone away,
> Gone far away into the silent land;
> When you can no more hold me by the hand,
> Nor I half turn to go yet turning stay.
> Remember me when no more day by day
> You tell me of our future that you plann'd:
> Only remember me; you understand
> It will be late to counsel then or pray.
> Yet if you should forget me for a while
> And afterwards remember, do not grieve:

For if the darkness and corruption leave
A vestige of the thoughts that once I had,
Better by far you should forget and smile
Than that you should remember and be sad.

I love that poem and it is something that I would wish for my children when I die. I want them to be happy, but I can hear my ego whispering, *How will they possibly manage without me?*

I do not think of joining Peter in heaven or anywhere else but I do contemplate death. It's only right when you get to my age.

I remember in my teens becoming physically sick thinking about death. I talked about it with my mother. She said that when you get old and your body is letting you down, the thought of dying isn't so bad. I didn't believe her then and I'm struggling to believe her now.

There are parts of my body that are aching (that bloody arthritic knee) and my sight is hanging on by an eyelash. I have to exercise my shoulder every day, which thankfully involves lifting a full glass of wine to my lips. So, yes, Mother, my body is letting me down, but I'm not ready to go yet.

Incidentally, if there is anyone under seventy reading this, I would recommend that you look after your feet and your teeth to achieve good health in old age.

And keep a diary. I have lots of memories in my pink

box but only two diaries. The first is for the year 1979, the year before my husband died, and the other for 1993, which says on the front cover ALL MEN ARE BASTARDS!!! I don't know who gave me that, maybe I bought it myself. This was the year I was studying for my Leaving Certificate and there are lots of entries about how economics was 'incomprehensible' and how I was 'sick of school'.

In both of those diaries, there is a consistent theme of how much I weighed, how much I should lose, what I must eat and not eat. I am sad reading those entries now and remembering all those years of 'watching' my weight. From the age of ten, when my school 'friends' called me Tugboat Annie, I have been at it. My parents worried and took me to the doctor, who prescribed half a tablet of Dexedrine a day and lots of raw carrots. I took diet pills prescribed by various doctors for many years. Eventually the medical profession stopped doling them out and I stopped taking them. But I have never stopped worrying about my weight. Only yesterday, I said to my housemates, 'I'm going to give up cakes and biscuits for Lent.' I don't believe in God, never mind Lent, but the worries are still there in the back of my mind at eighty-one years of age. I can't shake it off, it's an affliction. Don't worry, though, I'll probably be making an apple crumble on Sunday and eating it.

The great composer Shostakovich, who suffered ill health throughout his life, said:

We should think more about it and accustom ourselves to the thought of death. We can't allow the fear of death to creep up on us unexpectedly. We have to make the fear familiar, and one way is to write about it . . .

That's what I am doing, writing about it.

I had an experience which led me to believe that I already know what it's like to be dead. I went on a ten-day Vipassana meditation course with three close family members in 2010. Vipassana means 'to see things as they really are'. It is one of India's most ancient meditation techniques. It is all about non-reaction. It doesn't matter how much pain you are in as you sit cross-legged on the floor – although, in fairness, they did give me a funny contraption to sit on because of my age. Your hands and legs fall asleep but no matter. You are instructed to be aware of the sensations in your body and scan your limbs in a specific order. The idea is that by doing this for ten days you train yourself to stop reacting.

On the first day, I was woken up at 4 a.m. ready for the meditation session at 4.30 a.m. where the focus was on learning how to breathe. At 6.30 a.m. there was break-fast, lunch at 11.00 a.m., tea at 5.00 p.m., which was just that – tea. During each of those ten days I was expected to meditate for ten hours, sometimes on my own and sometimes in the hall with everybody else.

For me, it was the Noble Silence requirement that was my downfall. Noble Silence means silence of body, speech and mind. Any form of communication with a fellow student, whether by gestures, sign language or written notes, is prohibited. I read all that in the leaflet beforehand but I didn't realize how it would affect me.

For the next ten days I was ignored. Ignored completely. It felt as if I wasn't there. I was invisible. To everybody. I hated every minute of it. And that's how I can say today that I think I know how it feels to be dead, even while consuming two hearty vegetarian meals a day.

It was after the retreat that I began to think more about death and how I would handle it when it came. The fact that we all have to die is quite shocking to me. My ego tells me it is preposterous. How could the world go on without me?

There are lines in the 3,000-year-old Indian epic *Mahābhārata* that go:

'What is the most surprising thing in the world?' a celestial figure asks a nobleman.

The nobleman replies: 'Day after day man sees countless people die but still he acts and thinks as if he will live forever.'

We will all die and talking about it can be beneficial so that we don't fall into the trap of pretending that our life will go on forever. That's how the Death Cafes came into being. I haven't been to one myself yet, but it seems to me to be a very good idea. People get together to eat cake, drink tea and discuss death in a cafe. Jon Underwood started the first Death Cafe in 2011 in the East End of London and now there are many in Dublin too. Their stated objective is 'to increase awareness of death with a view to helping people make the most of their (finite) lives'.

Friends think I am morbid when I recommend books about death such as *On Death and Dying* by the late Elisabeth Kübler-Ross or *Being Mortal* by Atul Gawande, which I have just finished reading and will be recommending to my children. Gawande writes about how people are treated in nursing homes, infantilized in many cases, and what can be done about it.

Over the years, I have read and reread *Memento Mori* by Muriel Spark. Nearly all the characters in the book are over seventy and an anonymous caller regularly telephones and says: 'Remember you must die.' One of the old girls says: 'It is difficult for people of advanced years to remember one should die. It is best to form the habit when one is young.'

The descriptions of their reactions to the phone call and the carry-on at funerals are hilarious. And yes, I agree with that premise, it is best to think about death when you are young and get it out of the way.

I recently purchased on Audible *A Tomb with a View*, the stories and glories of graveyards by Peter Ross. Surprisingly, I found it a very uplifting book. Ross talks a lot about Glasnevin Cemetery, which is very close to where

I live now. The cemetery covers 124 acres and holds 1.5 million graves, more than Dublin's current population. It is quite the tourist attraction since they did it up.

People in Ireland are very conscientious about tending and visiting graves but I am not that way. Peter is buried in Deansgrange Cemetery and since his death I have only been there once.

Mount Jerome Crematorium in Harold's Cross was once my preferred option for my funeral. It is favoured by agnostics and atheists because there is no official religious ceremony required. People say a few words about the departed, maybe read a poem or two, and there is usually music before the coffin disappears behind the curtains.

After tears and handshakes with the nearest and dearest, some go about their business, others go back to the home of the dead person or to the local pub for a bowl of soup. After one such cremation, I was invited to join the family in the RDS dining rooms where a splendid meal was consumed and many laudatory speeches made. Another time, there were canapés in the Merrion Hotel.

I loved the sense of occasion and after these events I said to whoever of my family might be listening that I would like to be cremated at a ceremony in Mount Jerome. I also reminded them that they would need to provide more chairs as I had noted that sometimes people had to stand. *Write it all down*, they said, *in case we get it wrong*.

With this in mind, I planned the funeral and the music

meticulously. 'Beautiful Boy' would be for my sons, 'Look Mummy, No Hands' sung by Camille O'Sullivan for my daughters, 'Girls Were Made to Love and Kiss' sung by Richard Tauber for Peter, and 'Wouldn't It Be Loverly' from *My Fair Lady* for myself. I intended to leave a list of my favourite poems from which they could choose. I imagined that I might even write a letter to everyone that could be read out at the ceremony. There would be masses of white roses everywhere. A big leather-bound book would be provided for signatures and fond memories. Afterwards, a wonderful picnic in Sandymount Green, weather permitting, catered for by Domini Kemp or whoever was available.

I think I must have been feeling very unwell when I was painting that scenario. Or maybe I was just carried away by the drama of it all. I have no desire to be the centre of attention in my day-to-day life – why then did I think it necessary when I was dead?

So I thought again. There will be no frills, I said. Straight to the crematorium, no eulogies, no music, and, most importantly, it would be carried out at minimum cost. I had heard of people spending thousands on funerals and I was determined that nobody would buy into a lavish and expensive send-off for me. There is a company that specializes in low-cost funerals, I told them, and you can get it all done for €890 including a cheap wooden coffin. I googled it.

Since then I have modified – nay, changed completely –

my ideas about my funeral yet again. Everybody is entitled to change their mind.

I watched the documentary made by RTÉ entitled *A Parting Gift*, which followed a year in the life of medical students learning from anatomical donations. Over a hundred people a year in Ireland donate their bodies to medical science and I wanted to be one of them. To medical and science students studying anatomy they are known as the 'silent teachers'.

And after due consideration I took action. In order to inform my children of my decision, I sent them an email. I didn't want anyone to try to dissuade me.

To Sarah, Eddie, Brian, Rachael, Peter, Róisín, Michael and Katie

17 January 2016

I hope I am not going to upset your Sunday dinner but I just wanted to let you know that on my death I will be donating my body to medical science via The Royal College of Surgeons or if they are full up to one of the other medical schools.

I have today signed a form and sent it off and they will return a photocopy to me in due course. The college will cover the cost of cremation and provision of an urn. The cremation will take place from 1–3 years after my death. All you do is contact them (01–4022260 during office hours and 01–4752326 outside office hours).

This will all be free and so no unnecessary money need be spent as there will be no funeral as such.

Now that is off my chest, I hope you are all well and I look forward to seeing as many of you who are around next weekend.

Love

Ann xxx

There was a flurry of phone calls asking if I was unwell and what had made me send such an email. It was obviously the wrong way to communicate my decision and I was sorry. I just wanted to get it out of the way without any discussion.

After seeing *A Parting Gift*, I watched another documentary, *Body Donors*. It follows two people who have donated their bodies to science, both before death and after. Now I know exactly what will happen to my body when the time comes.

So, no cremation, no burial for me. My body is now donated to science. I have never liked the idea of graveyards, I just don't see the point. I wouldn't want anybody to waste time and money on bringing flowers to put on a grave.

I want to live now for as long as I can (I'm aiming for one hundred) because, afterwards, there will be nothing. I have written about it, read about it and made my decision. All that is left is to face death with equanimity. Maybe I did learn something at that Vipassana course.

There's only one thing that bothers me and makes me sad: I will never know the end of the story.

Peter Ingle, 1939–1980

Acknowledgements

When you get to my age and you look back, there are so many people who have played an important part in your life. All those friends I made over the years in Sandymount, Irishtown, Ringsend and further afield are too numerous to mention. There would be another book to be written if I thought too hard or lingered too long. So, I am going to say if you ever gave me the time of day, listened to me, befriended me, worked with me, gave me the opportunity to earn a crust, made material contributions to the welfare of me or my children, I thank you.

When I came to live in Ireland, I was very fortunate to have been welcomed into the amazing Ingle family. Thank you all for being so kind as to accept this strange Englishwoman into your midst.

My sister, Joyce Dellar, and my sister-in-law, Eva Hutton, have been cheering me on from afar as I wrote this book. Your enthusiasm for my endeavours is greatly appreciated.

I never really imagined that I would turn into one of those 'ladies who lunch' but advancing years, retirement from work and a bit of extra cash did it for me. So to my friends June Finegan, Lou Trenaman, Valerie Hobson, Elizabeth McArthur and Annette Mulkern, I wish for all of us many more good meals together in the best of hostelries.

The many book club friends I have made have contributed to my extensive library. They have introduced me to volumes I would never have dreamed of reading so thanks to all of you, especially Eda Sagarra, Martina Quinn, Sean Gorman, Daragh Downes and Harry Woolfson.

I am grateful to the people who have helped me over the years to string words together, especially Susan Knight, Ian Ransom, Ivy Bannister, Eileen Casey and my fellow writers in the PS Writers Group. Thanks especially to Kaja Steinbuch for taking the time to read my initial long-winded attempt at a memoir and for giving me her candid and useful advice.

Writing a memoir is different from telling the life story of someone else, as I did with *Driven*. That began with a telephone call from Paul Howard. 'Rosemary Smith wants her life story written so I told her you could do it.' Thanks, Paul, for starting my professional writing career and for being the funniest man I know.

Faith O'Grady of the Lisa Richards Agency read reams of my memories before gently guiding me in the right direction. Your tactful forbearance is greatly appreciated.

Thanks to Penguin for publishing my book and to the team for all their good work. They came up with a delightful jacket in which to wrap my words. The photograph on the cover was taken at the wedding of Eileen and Michael Gemmel in 1970 and I am grateful to them for allowing me to use it.

I have a wonderful editor in Patricia Deevy. She asked me all the right questions and encouraged me in my endeavour to make this book the best it could possibly be. Thank you, Patricia, for those over-the-hedge chats.

Without the help of the National Council for the Blind of Ireland and the medical staff of the Royal Victoria Hospital my ability to see what I am writing would be severely diminished. Thank you for your care and kindness. Also I am indebted to Declan Meenagh for technical assistance with my smartphone.

I consider myself an extremely fortunate woman to have such splendid grandchildren. Each one of you brings me a unique and fresh view of the world and I thank you for keeping my eyes and mind open: Fionn Ruadh, Bláithín Ruadh, Mella Ruadh, Rossa Ruadh, Peter Ingle, Niel Ingle, Hannah Burgess, Emma Burgess, Daniel Burgess, Charlie Ingle, James Ingle, Joya Hobson, Priya Hobson, Joseph Ingle, Lucas Ingle, Síofra Ingle Holmes, Iseult Ingle Holmes and Mícheál Ingle Holmes (who provides the cuddles).

My children are a constant source of wonder to me and their words of encouragement and practical assistance during the writing of this book have been invaluable. So thank you Sarah, Brian, Eddie, Rachael, Peter, Róisín, Michael and Katie. I am especially grateful to Róisín for her unfailing belief in me, to Sarah for her eagle eyes, supplementing my own failing ones, and to Katie for keeping the show on the road.

I am happy to say that my children made admirable choices when it came to finding life partners. Willo Roe, Paul Burgess, Aoife Walsh, Rukhsana Kauser, Killian Holmes, Katy O'Kennedy and Jonny Hobson are not just in-laws but good friends and allies. Thanks especially to Killian for the pep talks and cups of tea, and to Jonny for his exemplary eye for detail.

Finally, to all those who have bought this book and taken the time to read it, I raise my glass. *Sláinte*.